Extraordinary Furniture

David Linley
Extraordinary Furniture

MITCHELL BEAZLEY

for Serena

Extraordinary Furniture

by David Linley

Contributing Editor Janet Gleeson

First published in Great Britain in 1996
by Mitchell Beazley,
an imprint of Reed Books
Michelin House, 81 Fulham Road, London SW3 6RB
and Auckland, Melbourne, Singapore and Toronto

Executive Editor Alison Starling
Executive Art Editor Vivienne Brar
Project Editor Anthea Snow
Designers Geoff Borin, Geoff Fennell
Text Editor Richard Dawes
Picture Research Wendy Gay, Clare Gouldstone
Production Controllers Jenny May, Heather O'Connell
Indexer Hilary Bird

A CIP catalogue record for this book is available
from the British Library

ISBN 1 85732 786 1

Set in Linotype Helvetica Neue and Linotype News Gothic
Produced by Mandarin Offset, Hong Kong
Printed in China

Title page **Sofa designed for the Casa Ibarz by Aleix Clapes
in collaboration with Antoni Gaudi c.1900.**

This page **Commode by Charles Cressent at Waddesdon Manor.**

Contents

Introduction

The starting-point for this book was my fascination with unusual and remarkable pieces of furniture. I hope that others will enjoy seeing and reading about them, for they are among the most enthralling objects ever made.

But what was I looking for in my quest? I approached the project much as one would a treasure hunt, and by picking up clues dropped by the many people who helped me along the way I unearthed an unexpected wealth of sumptuous, stylish, ingenious, and bizarre pieces of furniture. I make no pretence to be a furniture historian, yet I hope that by writing a book that focuses on these weird and wonderful pieces, and examining them in a fairly light-hearted, non-academic way, I might be able to interest and attract more enthusiastic amateurs like myself to a field that sadly still seems unfamiliar to most people. So began my hunt to find extraordinary pieces of furniture. To make the book as exciting as possible I deliberately chose many pieces that have rarely been seen and discussed outside specialist publications, and some that have never been shown in a book, or which, like the amazing 16th-century steel chair on pages 88–9, have never before, as far as I know, been photographed in colour. What makes a piece extraordinary can be a combination of factors and is often a matter of personal opinion. Rarity, design, craftsmanship, and materials are all such factors, and in some cases the pieces are extraordinary as much for the stories behind them as for their appearance.

On the pages that follow you will find my own personal selection of furniture that I found to be particularly intriguing, inspiring, and remarkable for one reason or another. I make no claim that this is a definitive list of the most outstanding pieces ever made. My research for the book has taught me that for every "extraordinary" piece I found, there was another around

Left **The Studiolo of Federigo da Montefeltro, in the Palazzo Ducale, Urbino, testifies to the remarkable skill of craftsmen of the Renaissance. Dating from the 1470s, this room was used to store manuscripts. The identity of the designer of the marquetry decoration remains a mystery, but it is believed that he collaborated with the architect Luciano Laurana.**

Right **This four-panelled sycamore screen by David Linley Furniture was inspired by the Studiolo. Inlaid with over thirty varieties of wood, it shows a three-dimensional effect created by shading the wood by dipping it in hot sand – a traditional technique known as sand-burning. The screen's musical theme reflects the profession of the client.**

the corner waiting to be discovered, and there are doubtless many that I have still to find.

Alongside remarkable furniture that has rarely been seen, I have also included some reasonably well-known and famous pieces that are displayed in public collections, and there is a guide on page 184 to where these can be seen. I also picked the brains of experts I met on my travels abroad and as a result I came across some remarkable objects. During a recent trip to Houston, Texas, I was taken round the outstanding collection at Bayou Bend by its generous curator, who opened the house specially for me. Two pieces from the assortment of American furniture displayed in this house are included in Chapter 2: Extraordinary Design. In order to make this personal selection more coherent I have grouped the pieces according to one of the prime reasons why they seem to me to be outstanding (in several instances pieces qualified for various categories).

Below **A client's elegant colonial home near New York was reduced to miniature size and fitted with hidden storage compartments to create a novel keepsake box.**

The Perspective of Patronage

During my career as a furniture maker and designer I have been greatly influenced and inspired by the many exceptional pieces with which I have come into contact. As I collected objects for the book I was therefore fascinated to find out more about the motives and inspirations of the makers of such objects, in terms of the prevailing styles and tastes and the people for whom they were made. I was intrigued by the way in which, in many cases, I could sense the personality of the owners so emphatically in the appearance of the pieces made for them.

This personal quality, which is inherent in most hand-crafted furniture, is partly what drew me to the subject in the first place. Furniture evolved to perform some practical purpose, and despite the incredible range of pieces that have been made over the centuries, nearly every piece you can think of falls into one of three categories: it provides something to sit or lie on, to store possessions in, or a surface on which to place objects. From the very earliest times furniture also became a way to reflect social status and power, but however complex its symbolism the human connection continued to exert a potent influence on its appearance. For example, the extraordinary

Dolphin Suite on pages 46–9 is made in the classically inspired Regency style fashionable at the time, yet the exuberantly carved fish that adorn it also reflect both the name and temperament of the generous Mr Fish for whom it was made. Similarly the Table of the Grand Commanders (*see* pages 154–5), which was commissioned by Napoleon and paradoxically ended up in the collection of his arch-rival George IV, is studded with victorious classical military leaders, revealing the French Emperor's own military aspirations. And I cannot look at the amazing *pietre dure* commode by Martin Carlin (*see* pages 104–5) without imagining the lovely courtesan and star of the Paris Opéra, Marie-Josephine Laguerre, whose elegant apartments it once graced. The stories of the individuals whose lives played a part in the commissioning of a piece, or even those who were its subsequent owners are, I feel, integral to our understanding and appreciation of it, and a theme on which I have concentrated wherever possible.

The importance of the patron is no less significant today than it ever was. I have noticed that when we are commissioned to make a piece of furniture. The time and effort a patron puts into talking to us, coming to the shop to choose the wood, and following the development of the piece in the workshop almost invariably has a dramatic effect on the end result.

Right **Detail of the sofa from the Dolphin Suite, made for Mr Fish c.1810 (*see* pages 46–9).**

Design and Inspiration

Furniture is something that is almost invariably created to work as well as to look good. My father, who played a crucial role in my own development as a designer, frequently reminds me of Anthony Trollope's description, in *Barchester Towers*, of Mrs Stanhope, who "well knew the great architectural secret of decorating her constructions, and never descended to construct a decoration" – a principle that can be applied to furniture design just as easily as to dress sense! As a designer-maker I have been fascinated by the way design, construction techniques, and craftsmanship combine to create such a wide variety of pieces that both work well and look pleasing.

Some of the most extraordinary and personally appealing pieces of furniture are those that combine two functions within one item. The various forms of library steps that evolved in the 18th and 19th centuries included some that could literally turn inside out and transform into a table and chair. Giovanni Socci devised a remarkable desk (*see* pages 132–3) for the demanding Elisa Bonaparte, Grand Duchess of Tuscany and sister of Napoleon. Not all such ingenious designs were great rarities. Examples of the patented table created by Robert Jupe in the early 19th century (*see* pages 138–9) appear from time to time in saleroom catalogues. Despite the fact that such pieces are not unique, I am no less enthralled by the mechanism that operates the iron ribs under the circular table and allows it to expand. This innovative design has also inspired an equally ingenious modern interpretation (*see* pages 140–1).

Many of the pieces I have included have great personal significance for me. As a child I was lucky enough to be taken to many houses by my mother and father, who always pointed things out and made me look carefully. I remember that on some of these excursions my father would just walk up unannounced to the door of an interesting house and ask politely if we could possibly look round – terrifying at the time but wonderful to look back on. Sometimes we played a game where, after looking around a house, we would close our eyes and describe the things we had just seen. That was a very good way to learn how to look and to remember.

While researching this book I revisited several collections of furniture that are open to the public. As I examined each piece I was struck by the fact that people passed so fleetingly through the rooms and devoted so little time to looking at the furniture. I hope that, by discussing in some detail each of the pieces I have chosen, others will find as much pleasure as I did in looking more searchingly at each extraordinary piece.

Left **Detail of the Sèvres porcelain top of the Table of the Grand Commanders (*see* pages 154–5).**

Below **Thomas Sheraton described this design for folding library steps, published in his *Drawing Book* 1791–4, as being first made for "the King and highly approved of by him, as every way answering the intended purpose".**

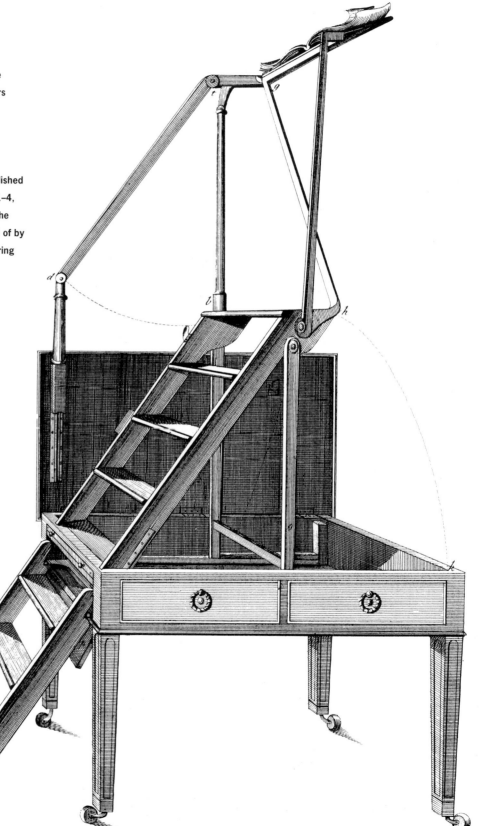

13

My own approach and response to the pieces I have chosen has, naturally enough, been governed by my fascination with both design and craftsmanship. These two qualities are fundamental for any noteworthy piece of furniture, ordinary or extraordinary, and have endlessly preoccupied furniture makers past and present.

When I started making furniture at school, it seemed that mass-production had won the day, hand-crafted furniture was, apart from the odd exception, in the doldrums, and almost no hand-inlaid furniture was being produced. In my early days I found tremendous satisfaction in cutting a joint and tightening the clamps to see the glue emerge and a perfect joint appear before my eyes. Then, at the end of term, I felt a great sense of fulfilment at having something to show for my earlier efforts. But now, when I look back at my earliest work with the benefit of hindsight, it seems to me very angular, very colourful – and very outrageous.

As I progressed I realized that I was in danger of falling prey to fashion in trying to invent new, ever more bizarre forms. And so I began to look back at designs of the past, and in this way I discovered history. I looked for pieces that had stood the test of time and tried to incorporate some of these ideas in my own work. As soon as I made the discovery that this reinterpretation of classicism was popular I began increasingly to concentrate on this style. As a result, our identity as a business began to emerge, and our brand of classical modernism has, over the years, become increasingly distinctive.

Many of our designs are inspired by ancient architecture, a source of inspiration that we share with furniture designers throughout history. The Duke of Atholl's medal cabinet (*see* pages 62–3) was based on a Roman landmark, cabinets were designed as Renaissance palaces in miniature (*see* pages 22–3), and the Linnells' famous bed made for Badminton House (*see* pages 56–7) resembled a Chinese pagoda.

In much the same way architecture has provided me with an important source of ideas. We started by taking Venetian architecture as our inspiration, using watercolour techniques to translate the jumbled façades into designs that we were able to apply to screens. The various veneers available to us we used in much the same way as an artist uses a palette of colours. From there we moved on to applying similar techniques to other forms of furniture.

Right **Detail of a Chinese-style bed, probably made by William and John Linnell c.1854 and forming part of a suite of furniture (*see* pages 56–7.)**

Below **Library writing table made by Thomas Chippendale and based on a Robert Adam design for Harewood House, Yorkshire, c.1770. The piece is veneered in rosewood and decorated with various exotic wood inlays and gilt metal mounts. (The matching library steps are shown on page 123.)**

14

Construction and Collaboration

From the earliest times many spectacular pieces of furniture (and certainly most of those featured in this book) were not the work of a single craftsman but the result of collaboration between designer and numerous specialists concentrating on crafts such as joinery, turning, carving, marquetry, stone inlays, painting, gilding, and casting metal mounts. Many specialist crafts still flourish, and in recent years the increased attention paid to restoration and conservation, as well as the revival of hand-craftsmanship, has regenerated interest in such skills.

Collaboration between various skills continues to play an important role in contemporary furniture making. All the pieces made by us and seen in this book result from collaboration between the patron, the design team, and specialist craftsmen. By employing traditional techniques and approaching each commission in a personal way, we are creating a link between the past and present. I hope to have underlined this sense of continuity by including pieces made by leading contemporary craftsmen alongside masterpieces of the past.

My fascination with wood is another reason why I decided to concentrate on becoming a furniture designer. In recent years we have chosen to try to limit the primary woods we use to three indigenous varieties: English oak, walnut, and sycamore. We occasionally use other timbers, and also use a wide variety in marquetry design, but these three woods are our trademark and have helped to give our furniture its characteristic identity.

Apart from wood, the huge variety of materials that can be incorporated in the construction and decoration of furniture is a subject that I also find fascinating; it is dealt with in Chapter 5: Extraordinary Alternatives. Glass, ceramics, paper, and textiles are just some of the materials that have been used. Our own designs too are beginning to incorporate increasingly varied materials, ranging from a folding chair in aluminium and canvas to one of our most ambitious pieces ever: a cabinet decorated with Sèvres porcelain plaques (*see* opposite page).

Looking through the incredibly diverse array of furniture in this book, I am filled with admiration and awe at the outstanding achievements of makers throughout the centuries. Most of the objects are beyond the realms of convention and many are completely irrelevant to modern living, and yet their exquisite craftsmanship, ingenious design, and eccentric approach to the problems and constraints of furniture making continue to inspire me. As you encounter these amazing pieces I hope you will experience the same sense of excitement, revelation, and pleasure that I did in discovering and learning about them.

16

Left Le Secretaire des Muses, an elaborate writing desk adorned with Sèvres porcelain plaques provides an outstanding example of successful collaboration between various craftsmen. Three secretaires of this type were made; this one dates from 1827 and the central panel was painted by Charles Etienne Leguay.

Right Inspired by English and French architecture and a desire to celebrate craftsmanship on both sides of the Channel, David Linley Furniture designed this cabinet in collaboration with Sèvres. The French factory is making the porcelain plaques for the façade – the first time it has made a plaque for furniture for a century and a half.

17

Extraordinary Extravagance

furniture of remarkable opulence and grandeur

Throughout the history of furniture certain pieces have stood out simply because of their overwhelming scale or the breathtaking opulence of their decoration. Time and money were no barriers to their creation, for many took years to complete, at astounding cost. Symbolic of their owners' status, wealth, and power, these unique objects were intended to overawe the viewer with their sheer beauty and their remarkable extravagance.

Left **Extravagance taken to extremes was the speciality of Pietro Piffetti, who constructed this cabinet in the Palazzo Reale, Turin, in 1731. Among the various materials that were used to create this dazzling piece are ivory, gilded metal, mother-of-pearl, and numerous varieties of wood.**

The Sea Dog Table

Feet in the form of plodding tortoises hold up pillars intricately carved as winged sea dogs. But what is the significance of the strange mythical creatures depicted in this fantastically carved walnut table? The piece is, in fact, not just an item of furniture but also a visual pun. The tortoises and winged hounds are thought to refer to the old adage Festina lente ("Hasten slowly"). But the wonder of the Sea Dog Table lies in its expressive carving, which makes it one of the most imaginative examples of Elizabethan furniture in England.

Below **This portrait of Elizabeth of Hardwick, Countess of Shrewsbury, was painted in the 1590s, after the death of her fourth and final husband.**

Top **When extended, the Sea Dog Table's leaves provided a surface on which to display treasures stored in a walnut cabinet of similar date which stands in the same room.**

Above **Among the most impressive of Elizabethan mansions, Hardwick Hall has a dramatic skyline adorned with the initials of Bess of Hardwick, for whom it was probably built by Robert Smythson.**

The Sea Dog Table is one of the few pieces of furniture from the Elizabethan era still to grace Hardwick Hall, ancestral home of Elizabeth, Countess of Shrewsbury, better known as Bess of Hardwick. The precise origins and early history of the table are unknown, but it is thought to have been made in England or France in the later decades of the 16th century. Its bizarre design is based on engravings published c.1560 by the French Huguenot architect Jacques Androuet du Cerceau I.

The table is a hotchpotch of eccentric detail. The dogs, with their quizzical, furrowed faces, have forepaws muscled like human arms that end in weird webbed feet. Their backs are covered in leaves that metamorphose into scaly, writhing fishes' tails. Beneath the plinth on which they rest, the four tortoises are splayed out, their heads poking up in grim determination, as if overwhelmed by the weight above them.

It is appropriate that one of the most compelling pieces of furniture of the Elizabethan period should have belonged to an equally forceful woman. Shrewd, extravagant, and ambitious, with a penchant for political intrigue, Bess of Hardwick was one of the most magnetic characters in a colourful age. Born in Hardwick in 1527, she spent her early adulthood in service in a large Tudor household. She married four times, and on each occasion significantly improved her financial fortunes and social status. Her final coup came in 1567, when she married George Talbot, 6th Earl of Shrewsbury and head of one of the most distinguished dynasties in England.

However, the marriage proved to be an unhappy one, for the Earl disapproved of the substantial sums of his money that his wife spent on Chatsworth, the ancestral home that formed part of her inheritance from her second marriage. She, meanwhile, fuelled gossip that her husband was romantically involved with Mary Queen of Scots. The Earl had been appointed Mary's custodian by Elizabeth I in 1569, and talk of this sort can scarcely have furthered his political career. It was probably the breakdown of the marriage and the wrangling over Chatsworth that led Bess to settle in her own property at Hardwick, where she had the old house pulled down and Hardwick Old Hall built in its place.

On her husband's death in 1590 Bess once again inherited vast tracts of land and a generous income. At the age of sixty, finding herself phenomenally wealthy, she set about building herself another splendid residence. Over the following decade Hardwick Hall took shape next to Hardwick Old Hall, to become one of the most impressive of Elizabethan mansions.

In the Withdrawing Chamber, at the centre of the grand suite of reception rooms that took up much of the first floor, the Sea Dog Table had pride of place. It was probably originally partly gilded and when in use it was covered by a rich needlework cover embroidered with "the storie of David and Saule with a golde frenge and trymmed with blewe taffetie sarcenet".

Inventories of 1601 described "a drawing table carved and guilt standing upon sea doges inlayde with marble stones and wood". The table has a top inlaid with pieces of marble, and sliding sections that can be drawn out from underneath to extend its surface area – hence the term "drawing table".

Dogs held special significance for the Talbot family since the word "talbot" denotes a breed of dog, and dogs appear in the family insignia. In this case, though, the dogs are transformed into chimeras, fanciful creatures fondly described by the 6th Duke of Devonshire in the 1840s as "dogs with bosoms and dolphins' tails, with garlands round their necks and ostrich feathers instead of ears".

Above **The Sea Dog Table's carving is so fine that it may have been made originally for a member of the royal family.**

21

Italian Tortoiseshell Table Cabinet

Above **The central arch of the proscenium of Palladio's Teatro Olimpico makes the street seem to stretch into the distance. The theatre, begun in 1580, was Palladio's last work.**

Imagine turning a corner and seeing a palace, its façade adorned with tortoiseshell, ebony, ivory, and gilded statues, with receding arches that seem to stretch for ever. That is the impression that this remarkable cabinet creates when you see it for the first time, although in reality much of its impact is illusory. Made c.1650 in Naples or Rome, the piece is a product of an age when such objects embodied the wealth, learning, and power of their owners and mirrored the architecture of the grand palaces in which they stood.

The cabinet makes little pretence at practicality, for while there is storage space in the frieze and plinth and behind some of the arches, its main function is not as a cupboard. It is meant to be a visual extravaganza, dazzling in its sumptuous decoration and daring in the perspective games it plays with the spectator.

Architects of the baroque period were gripped by curiosity about perspective and loved to create a sense of drama by manipulating distance and scale. One of the most famous examples to excite their interest was the Teatro Olimpico at Vicenza, a theatre based on ancient Roman plans, which was designed by Palladio and finished by Scamozzi in 1581. Palladio's stage design gives the impression of great depth by intensifying the architectural perspective he creates. Floors tilt upward and corridors contract to make you think the stage stretches back much further than it really does.

This cabinet is designed to work in much the same way. If you look at it from the side you can see how the balustrade above the central arch dips down at a moderately acute angle. Similarly, the chequered floor is not flat but slopes up, the coffered ceiling slopes down, and the sets of columns are not the same size as those in front; nor are they placed behind them, but slightly inside. So as you stand and look at the cabinet from a distance, you think you are seeing beyond the façade into a palace of great depth. In fact, the piece is only 22in (56cm) deep – a modest size considering that it is over 6ft (183cm) wide and 51in (130cm) high.

Right **Cabinets on a grand scale were a specialty of craftsmen in 17th-century Naples and Rome. In this case, tortoiseshell was combined impressively with ebony and gilded bronze mounts.**

Below **At the cabinet's side, a hinged panel allows a view, apparently through its entire length, which is provided by a series of mirrors.**

The cabinet was probably meant to be placed on a specially made stand that would have allowed you to see it at exactly the right height for its optical gimmicks to have maximum impact. The design is loosely based on Michelangelo's Palazzo dei Conservatori in Rome. The central element in the baroque façade is an arch flanked by smaller niches to either side. Each opening finishes in an apse that would almost certainly originally have held a statuette.

As you approached you would have marvelled at the lavishness of the gilt bronze mounts. The balustrade, frieze, and plinth are studded with sixty-six plaquettes, each cast with a different historical or mythological scene. Posing precariously above them are gilded figures drawn from classical mythology and representing classical deities and the Liberal Arts. To the

refined spectator of the mid-17th century, each scene and each statue would have been instantly identifiable and would have combined to convey an allegorical message. The plaquettes depict stories from Ovid's *Metamorphosis*, Virgil's *Aeneid*, and Livy's *History of Rome*. The diminutive but detailed scenes include the Rape of the Sabine Women, the story of Romulus and Remus, the Rape of Lucretia, and several of Perseus's exploits. These exquisitely made plaquettes are cast in low relief from gilded bronze, and along with the balustrading, sculpted figures and other metal mounts, were probably made in the Augsburg region of southern Germany, an area famed for its high-quality metalwork, and for showpiece cabinets.

The other materials with which the cabinet is decorated also signal its importance. The piece is constructed from a pine

carcass, veneered in tortoiseshell, ebony, and ivory – some of the most precious materials available to the cabinet-maker at the time. Ebony, the principal wood used, was an expensive import from Africa or the East Indies; its hardness, distinctive blackness, and resistance to warping made it particularly popular with 17th-century cabinet-makers. Often it was combined with ivory, or inlaid with semi-precious stones. In this case the chequered floor of the cabinet, made with alternating squares of ebony and ivory in imitation of tiles, creates a striking effect.

Tortoiseshell was another highly sought-after material used for veneering expensive objects in the 17th century. This semi-translucent substance was distinctively marked with cloudy striations and in fact came not from tortoises but from marine turtles. In the hands of the 17th-century craftsman it was

24

a very versatile material. When exposed to heat, it became malleable, allowing separate sections to be welded together, moulded into circular forms, or used to simulate low-relief carving. Here, tortoiseshell has been used in a great variety of ways. The foremost columns have been veneered with tortoiseshell treated to simulate fluting, while the bases have been pressed into battle and mythological scenes, including the Rape of Europa, as if they were miniature versions of Trajan's Column, the Roman landmark. Columns farther back have been spirally moulded and flat pieces of shell have been applied throughout the cabinet's façade to provide a contrast with the black ebony and a suitably rich foil to the sumptuous gilt mounts.

When you had admired the decorations and negotiated the mythological maze, you might have been shown some of the precious objects the cabinet contained. The gilded plaquettes decorating the wide frieze beneath the balustrade centre six hinged panels which open to reveal banks of three drawers, and, in the centre, a larger compartment with a shallow tray. These would almost certainly have been used by the 17th-century owner of the cabinet to store precious coins, medals, and antiquities, which would have been taken out to show favoured guests. The dividing frieze, and recesses in the main section below, conceal more drawers, while the plinth on which the cabinet stands also has a series of drawers, each embellished with gilded plaques.

Viewed from the side, the cabinet reveals further novelties. The side panel in the main section opens to reveal stretching before you a mirrored corridor that runs the whole length of the cabinet. Or does it? With this piece you are never sure whether what you see is real or created with mirrors – and therein lies much of its dramatic power.

Left **Four gilded musicians are seated on top of the four pairs of columns that support the front of the façade.**

Left **A surprising number of storage compartments are concealed within the cabinet. These may have related to the subject-matter of the plaquettes with which the piece is generously decorated.**

The Knole Silver Suite

A rare survivor from the baroque period, this sumptuous set of silver furniture was made for Frances, Countess of Dorset, who was one of the wealthiest heiresses of the 17th century. The glittering impression that it creates results from the fact that the silver's reflective qualities have been exploited to the full. Barely a scrap of surface is not intricately chased, and in the dimly lit room in which the pieces were intended to stand, the raised decoration amplified light and shade, producing an effect as dramatic as any theatre spotlight.

Above **Knole, a rambling Tudor mansion, was built between 1456 and 1486 by Thomas Bourchier, Archbishop of Canterbury. Queen Elizabeth I presented the great house to her cousin, Thomas Sackville, 1st Earl of Dorset, in 1566, and it has been occupied by his descendants ever since.**

Judging by portraits of her, Frances was a remarkably beautiful woman. The mother of thirteen children, she appears in a Van Dyck portrait hanging at Knole ravishingly serene in a satin gown. Frances was the daughter of James I's powerful minister, Lionel Cranfield. Her first husband, Richard Sackville, 5th Earl of Dorset, died in 1677 and left Frances mistress of Knole, in Kent, one of the most splendid houses in Britain.

This suite was probably bought by Frances to celebrate her second, slightly less advantageous marriage in 1679 to Henry Powle, Master of the Rolls. Although it has certainly been in its present surroundings for nearly three centuries (in 1706 the suite was listed in an inventory of the King's Room), it may originally not have been intended for Knole at all, for Frances also owned two other substantial houses: Copt Hall in Essex and a residence in London. The fashion for silver furniture was one that had first flowered in the court of Louis XIV. However, the French melted down most of their silver furniture to raise money for wars. This suite is one of only two complete surviving sets of English silver furniture known. (The other resides in the State Apartments at Windsor Castle.)

If you visited a bedchamber in a grand house in the 17th century you would probably have found that, in addition to a grand bed, it would be furnished with a looking-glass, table, and candlestands. These were typically all placed against a wall between two windows, and a silver toilet service, consisting of jewel caskets, boxes of cosmetics, hair and clothes brushes,

Left **Lady Frances Cranfield, portrayed here by Van Dyck, was heiress to the Earl of Middlesex, Lionel Cranfield. In 1679, two years after the death of her husband Richard Sackville, 5th Earl of Dorset, she married Henry Powle, Master of the Rolls. The furniture was probably made to celebrate this second union.**

Right **The silver mirror, table, and candlestands reside in the King's Room at Knole. The hallmarks on the candlestands indicate that they were made in 1676; the unmarked mirror probably dates from around the same time. The table bears a London hallmark of 1680-1.**

and scent flasks, would be laid out on a cloth on the table. The cloth was originally known by the French term *toile* – hence "toilet". As dressing rooms and closets became much more common later in the century, the traditional set of furniture, perhaps made from lacquer or inlaid wood, was included more as a form of decoration than for use. Silver furniture like this was the apogee of bedroom opulence, and a powerful way to display wealth to a visiting dignitary.

A wonderful combination of curving and scrolling shapes graces the components of the suite. The table, the largest and most elaborate piece in this suite, has legs formed from out-stretched "S" shapes and inward-swooping stretchers that are crowned in the centre with a wonderful baroque finial. Its top is decorated in characteristic baroque style with a central oval plaque that depicts a classical scene. The subject is Marsyas, the legendary flute player who challenged the god Apollo to a musical contest. Apollo won, and punished Marsyas by tying him to a tree and flaying him alive. All the woodland gods and animals mourned Marsyas and as they wept their tears created the River Meander.

The legend was a popular one with artists and sculptors of the period and this particular scene is based on an engraving published in Amsterdam in 1606. Surrounding this central plaque and adorning all the surfaces of the other components of the suite are richly chased baroque decorations. Scrolling acanthus leaves and putti, fruit, and flowers create a dazzling jungle of decoration that, in the dim, oak-panelled, tapestry-hung room, is still a breathtaking sight.

Above **The three "ginger jars", decorated with birds and flowers and also displayed in the King's Room, were made between 1685 and 1690, soon after the silver furniture.**

Casket on Stand
by Pietro Piffetti

Definitely not for the faint-hearted, this fantastically decorated casket on a stand is a small but virtuoso example of the work of Pietro Piffetti, an outstanding Italian craftsman whose name is justly synonymous with riotous rococo excess. The casket, which Piffetti made c.1745, takes the form of an aquatic extravaganza: the surface of both elements is encrusted with scales of mother-of-pearl laid in rippling lines, while the casket itself is shaped like a giant shell emerging from a pearl-petalled waterlily.

Presiding over the whole extraordinary concoction is the brass figure of Minerva, Goddess of Wisdom and War, who holds her Medusa mask in one hand and spear in the other. In front of her, cannonballs, a drum, a quiver of arrows, and a flag – trophies of war – lie scattered about. The edges of the shell casket are embellished with bands of brass rococo ornament simulating waves and rippling water, and, seated on the stand and holding up the casket, mer-figures on turtles hold dolphin tails in one hand and garlands in the other.

The stand beneath the casket is adorned with a similar lack of restraint. The rim has the same rippling metal decoration interspersed with shells and dolphins, and the curving cabriole legs have feet with metal mounts modelled as Indian heads, while an upcurving stretcher is decorated with Minerva's dragon and her helmet and arrows.

The extravagance of the gilded mounts contributes greatly to the impact of the piece and may be the work of Francesco Ladatte, Carlo Emanuele's bronze sculptor. Ladatte had trained in Paris and his elegant and sophisticated work reflects the influence of contemporary French *bronziers*.

In its curvy form and excessive decoration, this casket epitomizes the extremes of rococo style which Piffetti made his speciality. As yet the casket's full history remains untraced, although in 1780, two years after Piffetti's death, it is thought to have featured in a lottery organized by his nephew in Turin. A native of Italy's Piedmont region, Piffetti was born in 1700 and

Above **This elaborately inlaid cabinet from the Palazzo Quirinale in Rome reveals Piffetti's love of complex mounts and lavish curvilinear form. His later work grew increasingly restrained in style and shape.**

Right **The sensuous curves and asymmetrical motifs that form Piffetti's bizarre casket and stand are characteristic of the rococo style that dominated the applied arts throughout Europe between about 1740 and 1760.**

trained in Rome. By the age of thirty his virtuoso talents had come to the attention of one of the most powerful Piedmontese noblemen, the Marchesa l'Ormea, who enticed him back to Turin. A year later Piffetti was appointed royal cabinet-maker to the King of Sardinia, Carlo Emanuele III. Apart from brief spells in Rome in the 1740s, Piffetti is thought to have spent most of the rest of his career in Turin, where much of his time was devoted to embellishing royal buildings.

In the 18th century, Turin, the capital of Sardinia and Savoy, was a handsome town visited by many grand tourists. Piffetti, working with the Sicilian baroque architect Fillipo Juvara, was employed to decorate and furnish the king's residence, the Palazzo Reale. His work there was so outlandish that it almost defies description – not to mention gravity. Massively curling cabinets encrusted with lashings of spaghetti-like inlay and equally generous helpings of intricately chased-gilt mounts were suspended on bases which appeared impossibly fragile. As with this casket, there is barely a straight line to be seen in all Piffetti's work, and never a surface that is left undecorated. The effect, although it may not be to everyone's taste, is undeniably one of dazzling complexity, and displays a delightful disregard for the notion of restraint.

Right **The quality of the gilt bronze mounts suggests that they may be the work of the leading Piedmontese sculptor Francesco Ladatte, with whom Piffetti often collaborated.**

29

Italian Throne Seat by Antonio Corradini

What happens when an accomplished sculptor turns his hand to furniture making? In this case the result was a writhing mass of scantily clad female figures, twirling putti, stampeding horses, scrolls, and foliage that also happens to be a chair. Antonio Corradini, indisputably one of Venice's leading sculptors, is widely believed to have been the designer of this sumptuous throne seat that in many ways epitomizes the unashamedly excessive sculptural style of late-baroque furniture.

Above **A gilded console table as opulent in style as the gilded throne chair is also thought to be the work of Antonio Corradini. Many of the exuberantly sculpted motifs and figures, such as the shells, scrolls, central putti, and female caryatids, are similar to those adorning the chair.**

Made in Venice c.1730, this throne seat, along with a matching console table, is among the most outstanding pieces of furniture to be found in one of Venice's most beautiful palaces, Ca' Rezzonico. Sculptural furniture was to be one of the great strengths of Venetian furniture makers throughout the centuries (*see* also pages 166-9) and carved gilt wood became especially popular during the showy baroque period.

A chair like this was made by carving the frame from a soft wood such as pine, then coating the carved wood with several layers of gesso, a fine, chalk-like substance that could be rubbed perfectly smooth to create a suitable base for gilding. The prepared base was then covered with a layer of bole, a coloured clay, and when the clay was wet sheets of gold leaf were applied over the top. The shiny appearance was achieved by rubbing or burnishing the gold leaf with a hard implement – traditionally an agate.

Whether gilding is carried out or not, baroque style is invariably synonymous with drama and theatricality. Practicality was not a major consideration. This is a chair that wants to impress and astonish you – it is not for sitting in comfortably – and even now, two and a half centuries later, it still succeeds. Corradini has characteristically used every available surface to show off his skill. Sinuously twisting figures decorate the frame and are carefully posed to create a spiralling visual effect that carries the eye up to the central cartouche at the back. Unlike most chairs, however grand, the carving is not symmetrical;

Left **The façade of the Ca' Rezzonico, designed by Baldessare Longhena, was begun in 1667 and the top floor was added in 1752 by Giorgio Masari. The numerous columns, arches, and rusticated ground floor create a play of light and movement that is characteristic of baroque architecture.**

while the figures on either side balance each other, they are not identical. Like a director of a grand stage production, Corradini used a variety of poses in a visual game calculated to keep his audience captivated.

Antonio Corradini (1668–1752) was one of a number of leading sculptors who could turn their hand to furniture design when required to do so. This flamboyant piece and the matching table reflect the dramatic furniture styles pioneered in the work of Andrea Brustolon (1662–1732), another exceptionally skilful sculptor who was working in Venice at that time.

A contemporary of the talented Brustolon, Corradini was born in the Italian town of Este, and trained as a sculptor in Venice. Corradini rose to fame for his distinctive revivalist late-mannerist style – he was particularly fond of carving veiled statues. A sculpture for the Sansevero chapel in Naples entitled *Modesty* was carved from marble with such virtuosity that the veiled figure seems to be visible through the gauzy fabric. Throughout his career Corradini travelled extensively, working in Italian centres such as Venice, Rome, and Naples (where he died) as well as in other European cities, including Vienna, where he worked for Emperor Charles VI and stayed for ten years, Prague, and Dresden. His workshop in Rome, which was established after he settled there in 1740, is recorded as having been visited by the Old Pretender, James Edward Stuart, the exiled son of James II, as well as the Pope.

The palace of Ca' Rezzonico, where this and numerous other outstanding pieces of Venetian furniture provide such suitably sumptuous furnishing, was designed and begun by Venice's greatest baroque architect, Baldessare Longhena, in the 1660s. Longhena is most famously responsible for the design of Santa Maria della Salute, one of Venice's best-known churches, but the façade of the Ca' Rezzonico typifies the sculptural movement and monumental proportions of baroque architecture at its most successful. It is entirely appropriate that this splendid example of 17th- and 18th-century architecture should still be adorned with some of the finest pieces of furniture ever made in Venice.

Right **The amazing gilded throne seat by Antonio Corradini exemplifies the most expensive and most luxurious furniture made in Venice in the early 18th century. Such showpiece creations added greatly to the lavish interiors in which they were displayed, as this one does in the Venetian palazzo the Ca' Rezzonico.**

31

The Badminton Cabinet

The largest and grandest baroque cabinet created by the renowned Grand Ducal workshops in Florence, the Badminton Cabinet is among the most important pieces of furniture ever made. Remarkably, this outstanding piece was commissioned by the Duke of Beaufort when he was only eighteen years of age. But Henry, 3rd Duke of Beaufort (1707–45), was no ordinary eighteen-year-old. At the tender age of seven he had succeeded to one of the most powerful and illustrious dukedoms in England.

Right **The Badminton Cabinet is not only one of the most magnificent pieces of furniture ever made – it is also the most expensive, having been sold in 1990 for £8,580,000.**

Above **Badminton House, the ancestral home of the Duke of Beaufort, had been in the Somerset family since 1612. Extensively rebuilt in the late 17th century, the north façade, seen here in a painting by Canaletto, was based on part of John Webb's design for Somerset House in London.**

Right **A detail of one of the panels of *pietre dure* which decorate the central drawers of the cabinet shows how each was constructed from carefully selected semi-precious stone inlays. Birds and flowers were popular subject-matter for this type of decoration.**

After an initial education at Westminster and New College, Oxford, like many young aristocrats of the day the Duke set off on the Grand Tour, with his tutor, William Phillips, in tow. The tour not only put the finishing touches to his education, but also allowed him to buy a huge number of works of art: pictures, furniture, and antiquities. In doing so, he revealed himself as one of the grandest patrons of the day – a man not only of financial substance but also of superior learning and refined taste.

The Badminton Cabinet was probably commissioned in the spring of 1726, when the Duke visited Florence for a few days. It was made to take pride of place in a specially constructed "cabinet room" at his country seat, Badminton House, in Gloucestershire, where it was to be surrounded by Italian paintings, some of the other trophies picked up on his travels. The Florentine Grand Ducal workshops were well established as the leading centre of *pietre dure* – decorations made from semiprecious and hard-stone inlay. The workshops had been set up in the late 16th century by the dukes of Medici, on the first floor of the Uffizi, to produce works of art for the court.

By the 18th century the workshops, known as the Galleria, still did not take private commissions from anyone who just happened along, but in this case the Duke's social status and political contacts, as well as his family's sympathy with the Jacobite cause, probably helped him to gain access to the exclusive skills deployed there. In its overall scale and in the size of the individual panels the Badminton Cabinet represents the Galleria's most remarkable achievement. Just over a decade after its completion the workshops closed down.

The massive piece, which measures 152in (386cm) high and 91in (231cm) wide, took about six years to complete, and around thirty specialist craftsmen and supervisors would have been involved in its construction. It was made in five separate sections and dispatched with watercolour drawings that were intended to help the Duke to assemble it correctly on its arrival in England in 1732 or 1733.

The cabinet consists of ten drawers and a central door concealing a removable section that contains three smaller drawers. The strong architectural design of the piece, and the striking contrasts of stone, ebony, and gilt bronze, are typical of the Florentine late-baroque style. Each of the intricate pictorial panels is separated from the next by pilasters and each is set within an ebony and gilt bronze surround. This allows each panel to be appreciated as a work of art in its own right as well as part of a monumental whole. A huge range of semi-precious stones, including lapis lazuli, amethyst, chalcedony, and agate, has been used to create the jigsaw pictures of birds, fruits, and flowers. Blues and reds purposely predominate – these are the colours of the Beaufort coat of arms seen above the clock and give the elaborate structure an impressive final flourish.

For all his wealth and the beautiful possessions with which he habitually surrounded himself, the Duke led a rather unhappy life. William Phillips, who had accompanied him on the Grand Tour, fraudulently helped himself to a number of his young employer's pictures and offered them for sale at an auction room. Realizing what was going on, the Duke had an injunction placed on the sale of his property. His marriage to Frances, daughter of Sir James Scudamore, a Herefordshire landowner, was similarly ill-fated. The union was childless and unhappy, and when Frances eloped with another married man divorce and scandal ensued.

A year later, in 1745, the Duke died at the age of thirty-eight and was succeeded by his brother. He was not, it seems, greatly mourned. Mrs Delaney wrote of his death: "He was unhealthy in his constitution and unhappy in his circumstances – though possessed of great honour and riches; his brother is qualified to make a better figure, and his wife I hope will prove an honourable and virtuous Duchess of Beaufort."

Left and below **Discrepancies between some of the decorative details in the drawings and the Badminton Cabinet itself suggest that the watercolours were executed before the piece was finished.**

Right **The Badminton Cabinet was originally intended to provide a focal point in the 3rd Duke's Cabinet Room. In 1903 it was moved to the Great Drawing Room, where it stayed until it was sold in 1990.**

Scala di Braccio due a Panno Fiorentine

The Murray Cabinet
by John Channon

English furniture can rarely hold a candle to its continental counterparts as far as lavish decoration is concerned, but this ornate piece, made c.1750, is an exception. The Murray Cabinet is thought to be the work of John Channon, an 18th-century cabinet-maker renowned for his use of elaborate metal mounts and brass inlay. One of the most imposing and sumptuous pieces of case furniture attributed to him, the Murray Cabinet is so called because it passed by descent to Sir William Keith Murray of Auchtertyre, Perthshire.

Right **Behind a brass-inlaid mahogany door, the central section conceals a surprising seventeen compartments, which are revealed by releasing hidden catches.**

Above **The dragons, mask, and scrolling foliage that decorate the upper section of the Murray Cabinet's doors are made from engraved brass. The design was most likely adapted from a contemporary engraving.**

Right **John Channon constructed the massive mahogany cabinet in three sections: base, cupboard, and cornice. The maker of the striking gilt mounts remains unidentified, although their outstanding quality suggests that they were the work of a highly skilled craftsman.**

36

Extensive recent research into the life of John Channon by Tessa Murdoch and John Gilbert, as well as an important recent exhibition, have focused attention on the achievements of this remarkable but hitherto little-known maker. The son of a maker of serge – a cloth for which Exeter was famed – John Channon was born in that city in 1711, and served his apprenticeship in joinery under Otho Channon (possibly his elder brother). By 1737 John Channon was recorded as working in London, and the sophistication of this and other attributable works shows that he was aware of fashionable English and French styles.

In London Channon must have come into contact with the designs of his contemporaries such as Thomas Chippendale, William Vile, John Cobb, and the Linnells (*see* pages 56–9). His elaborate metal-inlaid furniture and fondness for large pieces of complex, monumental form reflect the influence of German styles of furniture – Abraham Roentgen, father of David (*see* pages 40–1), was in London at that time – and also suggest knowledge of the designs of the French cabinet-maker André-Charles Boulle (*see* pages 94–7).

The cabinet is almost as remarkable for its design as for its decoration. The doors of the upper half are hinged halfway back so that there are storage pigeon-holes and drawers in the doors as well as in the central pigeon-hole – a very ingenious feature. The main storage area appears deceptively simple, but the cupboard in the centre has seventeen secret pigeon-holes that are gradually revealed as you trigger concealed catches

and remove sliding panels. The keys to the cabinet include metal spikes that are used to release the catches. The lower part looks like a conventional serpentine-fronted commode but this also is unusual. The top drawer is fitted as a writing desk with a writing slide and can be pulled forward so that the canted corner sections double as legs.

However, it is the decoration that makes this piece so awe-inspiring. The mounts are not just generous but of sensational quality, so that each individual element could stand as a work of art on its own. Two gilt brass figures crowning the cabinet are copies of well-known antique sculptures, one a replica of the Venus de Medici, the other the Faun in Rosso Antico. The latter caused a stir when it was excavated in the 18th century and copies of it made souvenirs for visiting Grand Tourists. In the centre the cresting incorporates many ideas borrowed from French rococo designs. A watery cascade overflows beneath the central scallop shell that crowns the cresting, while both sides are edged with a pot-pourri of shells and rocks.

The corner mounts are exquisite, with satyr and nereid masks on top of a medley of shells, cascades, and ribbons. Even the keyhole escutcheon (on the right-hand door) is a minor masterpiece. The leaf-shaped and elaborately engraved spring flap that covers it is opened by pressing on a secret place. Engraved brass inlay adds to the rich effect: winged dragons, satyrs, foliage, and classical goddesses might have fallen from a book of mythology on to the vast mahogany doors.

37

Above **The double-hinged doors contain additional storage compartments, while the lower section's upper drawer acts as a writing table.**

The Bureau
du Roi

One of the most important, famous, and expensive pieces of furniture ever made, the breathtaking "Bureau du Roi" was the brainchild of one of the most accomplished cabinet-makers of the 18th century, Jean-François Oeben. The magnificent desk was intended for the private office of Louis XV at Versailles. The final cost, 62,000 livres, was an astounding extravagance, even by the standards of that frivolous king, and the piece remains one of the outstanding reminders of the lavishness of the French court.

Right **The Bureau du Roi's curved legs and extravagantly naturalistic gilt-metal mounts were designed to reflect the rococo style of the room in which the desk was to stand. The majority of fashionable furniture of this date was increasingly restrained, in keeping with the growing taste for neoclassical formality.**

38

Top **The unrivalled splendour of the royal palace of Versailles was created for Louis XIV, the "Sun King", at a cost of nearly 66 million livres. Almost a century later the Bureau du Roi – likewise at outrageous expense – was made for his great-grandson Louis XV.**

Above **The *ébéniste* Riesener, having taken over Oeben's Paris workshop, sustained its success until the Revolution brought about his ruin.**

The son of a German postmaster, Oeben was born at Heinsberg in 1721. Having established himself as a journeyman *ébéniste* in Paris, he married into one of the leading furniture-making families in the French capital. After setting himself up as an independent craftsman in the Louvre workshop of Charles-Joseph Boulle (youngest son of André-Charles Boulle), Oeben established a reputation for exquisite marquetry and novel mechanical pieces. Madame de Pompadour, the celebrated royal mistress and doyenne of fashionable taste, became one of his best customers and he developed a line in ingenious mechanical tables (*see* also pages 118–19).

After Boulle's death Oeben moved to the Arsenal district of Paris, where his workshop, one of the largest of the day, employed a dozen or so apprentices, and he was able to produce pieces of luxury furniture by the score. By 1760 his reputation had grown to such an extent that he was pronounced "*ébéniste mécanicien du roi*" (cabinet-maker by royal appointment) and granted his most important commission: to produce a desk suitable for Louis XV's *cabinet*, or private office.

Unfortunately, Oeben did not live to see the desk completed, for he died in 1763, leaving his masterpiece still a shadow of its future glory. However, neither the business nor the desk was left to gather dust for long, for Oeben's head worker, Jean-Henri Riesener, took over the running of his late employer's workshop and four years later married his widow. By 1769, nine years after the commission had been awarded

Above **The opened desk looks simple enough, but the central section of the writing surface can be pulled forward to reveal a writing well and a backrest.**

to Oeben, the Bureau du Roi, finally complete, was signed by Riesener and delivered to the palace at Versailles.

Even in the grand setting of Louis' *cabinet* the desk must have caused a sensation. All the subjects of the marquetry panels were carefully chosen to highlight Louis' interests as a man of learning and his position as a powerful monarch. On the front of the cylinder were cartouches symbolizing lyrical and dramatic poetry and royalty; the back was decorated with marquetry panels representing Astronomy and Mathematics; and the sides with the attributes of the sea and war. The mechanics of the desk were equally awesome. A quarter turn of the key – in itself a work of art in the form of Louis' cipher of interlaced "L"s and a miniature enamel portrait of Louis – was all the king had to do to automatically open or close the cylinder and the drawers below. Inside were a series of compartments divided by gilded

classical caryatids, geometrically inlaid drawers, and a writing slide with a secret well in the centre concealing compartments and a book rest. Another ingenious mechanism allowed a housemaid to open the drawers containing ink-wells from the side when the front of the desk was still locked, so that ink could be replenished.

It was almost inevitable that such an important piece, embodying royal privilege and power, should suffer over the ensuing period of political unrest, and several alterations were made to the decorations of the desk to erase its royal emblems. The blue and white biscuit plaques seen today on each side replaced marquetry panels of the interlaced "L" cipher. The central cartouche of marquetry, which originally showed the attributes of monarchy, was changed and modifications were made to several of the mounts.

This piece is one of the earliest cylindrical desks to be made in France and the first to be made on such a grand scale. In a fashion-conscious centre such as Paris the form quickly caught on, and over the following decades cylindrical desks became the archetypal grand pieces of 18th-century French furniture. Found only in the most splendid surroundings, these objects bespoke status, wealth, and taste. A potent symbol of prestige, the Bureau du Roi long outlived France's political disruptions. During the 19th century the Empress Eugénie had the desk moved to her cabinet at Saint Cloud, where it attracted such international attention that three exact replicas were made. One, bought by the Marquess of Hertford, is still in the Wallace Collection today. The bureau itself finally found its way back to Versailles, where, despite its alterations and chequered history, it retains the power to dazzle and amaze.

Bureau Cabinet
by David Roentgen

Virtuoso mechanics and spectacular pictorial marquetry were David Roentgen's dual specialties and this bureau-cabinet ranks as a tour de force of complexity, containing the ultimate in elaborate mechanics and ornate marquetry. It is one of three similar cabinets made by Roentgen for royal patrons with a taste for ostentation. The first in the series was made for Marie-Antoinette's uncle, Prince Charles of Lorraine; the second, now lost, was sold to Louis XVI for the astronomical price of 96,000 livres – the 18th century's most expensive piece of furniture; and this, the third version, was made for King Frederick-William III of Prussia in 1779.

Above **In the bureau section of the piece marquetry figures of Harlequin and Isabella are among six characters from the Italian *commedia dell'arte*. The six figures appear in turn on two rotating turntables.**

It is ironic that a devout member of a sect who adopted a lifestyle of great simplicity should have become a monumentally successful producer of furniture of the most luxurious and complex kind. David Roentgen was a German cabinet-maker whose sophisticated furniture took Paris by storm and made him one of the most successful makers of his day. But he was also a member of a zealous religious sect called the Moravian Brotherhood. He had been raised and educated according to the group's strict rules in the community's heartland at Neuwied, near Koblenz, and despite the huge success of his business, he always adhered to his religious beliefs.

The style and scale of the bureau cabinet – it stands nearly 13ft (4m) tall – gives it incredible dramatic impact. It is littered with so many architectural details – urns, balustrades, pilasters, plinths, arches, and architraves – that it suggests a theatre rather than a piece of furniture. A domed top, like a baroque cupola, is capped with a gilt bronze figure of Apollo and surmounts a musical clock made by Peter Kinzing, a clock-maker with whom Roentgen often collaborated.

Beneath the clock is a central door decorated on the outside with a marquetry panel showing Athena attaching a miniature portrait of King Frederick-William III to a column. The exterior panels are all decorated with extraordinarily elaborate

Left **The *trompe-l'oeil* room which forms the centrepiece of the bureau cabinet's upper section has walls lined with marquetry furniture. The "floor" can be raised to provide a bookrest.**

Right **The varied scenes which decorate the outer panels of the cabinet, now in the Schloss Köpenick, Berlin, were chosen to suggest that the arts, science, and commerce would prosper under the king's rule.**

Far right **In this detail of the intricate marquetry design decorating the central panel, the goddess Athena attaches a miniature portrait of King Frederick-William III to a pillar.**

marquetry pictures. The subjects are based on designs by the artist Janarus Zick and show personifications of various arts and science and commerce. Unlike other *ébénistes* of the day, Roentgen did not create shadow and depth by artificially colouring, burning, or engraving the wood, but simply by using countless minute wooden pieces of finely graduated colour.

But the full thrust of Roentgen's wizardry only becomes apparent when you open the cabinet. Apart from its many secret doors and hidden compartments that pop open at the press of a button or the turn of a key – standard features in much writing furniture by Roentgen – there are some much more intriguing novelties. The door in the upper part opens to reveal a cupboard that is decorated as a miniature stage set. Elegantly furnished with tables, chairs, and mirrors, this room provides a visual pun – furniture within furniture.

Beneath the *trompe-l'oeil* cupboard more surprises are revealed. The bureau included a mechanism that indicated the movement of the planets and the time of day, while if you press a catch the theatrical cabinet comes finally to life and a cast of marquetry figures from the *commedia dell'arte* rotate two at a time on turntables to the tunes of the musical clock. One can imagine that a spectator seeing such marvels for the first time could hardly have prevented himself from applauding their performance as appreciatively as the audience at the end of a successful first night.

41

Jewel Cabinet by Jean-Henri Riesener

A series of three massive jewel cabinets were among the most astonishingly luxurious pieces of furniture made during the reign of Louis XVI. This masterpiece by Riesener is the second in the series, and was made c.1785 for Marie-Josephine, Comtesse de Provence, who was married to Louis XVI's younger brother, Louis-Xavier, Comte de Provence (enthroned after Napoleon's defeat as Louis XVIII). It must have provided a stunning focal point in her apartments in the Palais du Luxembourg in Paris.

Made from mahogany veneered on to an oak carcass and decorated with sumptuous gilt bronze mounts, the cabinet reflects a hybrid of baroque and "*goût grec*", the neoclassical style predominating at the court of Louis XVI. The heavy cresting with putti holding up the arms of the Comte and Comtesse harks back to the Badminton Cabinet (*see* pages 32–5), but the rectangular shape and decoration echo fashionable neoclassical forms. Like the third version made by Schwerdfeger (*see* pages 44–5), Riesener's cabinet was partly inspired by a cabinet now lost, designed by the architect Jean-François Bellanger and commissioned as a wedding gift for Marie Antoinette from her husband-to-be, the Dauphin (later Louis XVI), in 1770.

The identity of the maker of the gilt-bronze mounts remains a mystery, but their quality and crispness are awesome. The central door panel contains striking detail: naturalistic birds peck at sprays of laurel and flutter on a highly elaborate perch of scrolling foliage draped with festoons of flowers. Tazze on the top of the cabinet and vases between the legs are made from blued metal also elaborately adorned with gilt-bronze mounts. Inside the outer doors there are three compartments flanked by banks of eight small drawers on each side and two larger ones beneath. The front of each drawer is decorated with gilt-bronze festoons and sprays of foliage and flowers that thread luxuriantly around the elegant bow handles.

The Comte and Comtesse both had a reputation for extravagance and an insatiable appetite for expensive furniture.

Above **The Comtesse de Provence, flatteringly portrayed by JB Gautier-Dagoty, is shown pointing to a bust of her husband Louis-Xavier, which stands in front of a portrait of her father, the King of Sardinia.**

Left **Much of the decorative detail of the piece, including this elegant caryatid, reflects the late 18th century's growing interest in classical antiquity.**

Right **The cabinet's rich overall effect is created by the lavishly chased gilt-bronze mounts with which it is generously adorned. The cresting at the top features three putti supporting the arms of the Comte and Comtesse.**

The Comtesse was used to living in opulent surroundings, being the daughter of the King of Sardinia, whose palace in Turin was incredibly sumptuous (*see* pages 28–9, Piffetti Casket on Stand). But by all accounts she was unappealing in appearance and character. Small, with a large nose, bushy eyebrows which she hated plucking, and a partiality for wine, she seems to have been more interested in her female friends than in her husband, and had such disregard for personal hygiene that her father wrote to implore her to pay more attention to such matters.

During the revolution the Comte and Comtesse managed to escape from Paris on the same night that Louis XVI and Marie Antoinette made their ill-fated getaway and were recaptured. The remainder of Marie-Josephine's life was to be spent in exile. She never saw her husband return to France and regain the throne, dying in England, at Hartwell House near Aylesbury, Buckinghamshire, in 1810 from hydropsy.

The cabinet, like most of the Provences' possessions, was left behind in France and was seized by the revolutionaries in 1793. Three years later it was advertised for sale in order to raise money for the nearly bankrupt government. During the political turmoil the value of luxury furnishings plummeted and by 1809 the cabinet was again on the market. This time it was on offer to Napoleon for the sum of 30,000 francs, half what the owner maintained she had paid for it. Napoleon, whose tastes were for furniture that underlined his military achievements (*see* pages 154–5), was not tempted and refused to buy. Two years later he was offered the cabinet once again. The master of his household suggested the Riesener cabinet might be appropriate to furnish the royal palace at Saint Cloud; by now the Empire style had become emblematic of Napoleon's reign. "His majesty wants the new and not to buy old," was the imperial response.

In contrast to the fashion-conscious emperor, England's King George IV was less concerned with the vagaries of the prevailing taste. An avid Francophile and ardent collector of French royal furniture, he had much in common with the exiled French monarch. Both men loved furniture, art, and food (Louis XVIII was so large that he has been described as the fattest French king ever); both had made unfortunate marriages; and both shared a passionate hatred for Napoleon. As Prince of Wales George had met the future Louis XVIII while he was living in exile at Hartwell House, inviting him to the celebrations held to mark his Regency and making him a Knight of the Garter before he set sail for France in 1814. It was not surprising then that George seized the opportunity to buy the cabinet, paying 400 guineas for it, when, a decade after Louis had reclaimed his throne and a year after his death in 1824, the piece turned up at an auction in England. Now in the Queen's private apartments at Windsor Castle, it remains arguably the most outstanding example of French furniture in the Royal Collection.

43

Jewel Cabinet
by J-F Schwerdfeger

This flamboyant jewel cabinet, made for Marie Antoinette in 1787, was perfectly suited to a queen whose love of luxury was legendary. Produced by the enigmatic ébéniste J-F Schwerdfeger, this is the third of the grand jewel cabinets made for the court of Louis XVI. Like Riesener's version (see pages 42–3) it is based on the missing cabinet given as a wedding gift to Marie Antoinette by her husband-to-be.

Above **The lavish jewel cabinet was made to grace Marie Antoinette's apartments in the Palace of Versailles. This vast royal residence, built by Louis XIV, is seen here in a painting by an unidentified artist.**

Right **A view of the Queen's bedchamber, painted by JB Gautier-Dagoty, shows in the background a large cabinet which is of similar form to Schwerdfeger's jewel cabinet. This may be the missing cabinet which was made for Marie Antoinette as a wedding present from her future husband, and which inspired the design of the cabinet made by Schwerdfeger.**

Jean-François Schwerdfeger is one of the most mysterious *ébénistes* of the late 18th century. One of several craftsmen of German origin working in Paris at the time, he is known to have supplied luxurious furnishings for Marie Antoinette's bedroom at the Petit Trianon. He was clearly a brilliant craftsman, but only a very few rare pieces have been discovered bearing his stamp, of which this jewel cabinet is by far the most remarkable.

Marie Antoinette delighted in furnishings reflecting the burgeoning contemporary interest in antiquity. Accordingly, every surface of the mahogany cabinet is smothered with classical decoration, and numerous craftsmen must have been engaged to make such a plethora of ornaments involving such a variety of ingredients. There are lavish gilt-bronze mounts, probably chased by Pierre-Philippe Thomire, the leading Parisian *bronzier* (maker of bronze mounts), the most spectacular of which are the four classical caryatids that divide the panels and support the entablature. These are inspired by antique sculpture and represent the four seasons.

The strong rectangular shape, and the straight, tapering legs, also reflect the simpler shapes that became fashionable during the neoclassical period. Nonetheless, the design of the piece still contains elements of styles of the previous century. The dramatically gesturing group, representing Fame and attendants, that provides the cresting is depicted with baroque theatricality. It is easy to imagine that this flamboyance greatly appealed to a queen for whom dramatics and dressing up were a favourite pastime, and whose small palace, the Petit Trianon, contained a theatre built expressly so that she could put on plays with her friends.

In addition to these glittering ornaments there are also pseudo-antique cameos carved by Degault, another prominent craftsman, surrounding the central medallion and punctuating the frieze above; plaques made by the royal porcelain factory of Sèvres which take the form of classical low-relief carvings and also show the influence of Wedgwood's designs; and panels of *verre églomisé* (glass painted on the reverse) reflect frescos recently discovered in ancient Pompeian interiors.

The cabinet was made just as the Ancien Régime, represented by Marie Antoinette and Louis XVI, drew to a close, and storm clouds of revolutionary discontent were gathering. Two years after the presentation of this cabinet to the Queen by the City of Paris in 1787, the Revolution led to the destruction of the French monarchy. In view of the events to unfold, some of the decoration is rather poignant. The legs of the cabinet are decorated to look like groups of tied arrows. This is a classically inspired device: in ancient Rome bundles of wooden rods (*fasces*) bound by a cord were carried by attendants of the consul to symbolize his authority. The motif, used here to support a *tour de force* of royal furniture, implies the unassailable power of the monarchy. However, the same device reappeared later on furniture of the Empire period. The Table of the Grand Commanders (*see* pages 154–5), commissioned by Napoleon and later acquired by George IV, used the same device as a central support. More immediately, bundles of bound arrows were reincarnated as the emblem of the Revolutionary establishment that swept away France's ill-fated king and queen.

Left **The cabinet is thought to have been designed by Bonnefoy-Duplan, the superintendent of the Garde-Meuble, which supervised the furnishing of royal palaces.**

Above **JF Bellanger's design for the lost jewel cabinet inspired not only Schwerdfeger's piece but also Riesener's jewel cabinet for the Comtesse de Provence (*see* pages 42–3).**

The Dolphin Suite

A spectacular example of Regency flamboyance, this fish-adorned suite of furniture, consisting of a couch, four window seats, ten armchairs, a pair of card tables, a sofa table, a pair of firescreens, and a lamp, was made c. 1810 for the aptly named Mr John Fish. The luxuriantly decorated suite was a homage to Lord Nelson, who had died at the Battle of Trafalgar in 1805. The British naval supremacy established at Trafalgar had stirred strong national pride – not least in the heart of Mr Fish. Therefore, when Fish died, in 1813, his second wife presented the centrepiece lamp, in memory of Nelson, to Greenwich Hospital.

Right **The twenty-one-piece Dolphin Suite, loaned to the Royal Pavilion in Brighton by the trustees of Greenwich Hospital, is now displayed in an appropriately opulent Regency setting in the Music Room.**

Above **One of the pair of rosewood card tables with brass-inlaid tops that form part of the Dolphin Suite. The pedestal in the form of four giltwood fishes reflects the suite's maritime theme.**

Right **This engraving, partly printed in colour, shows John Fish in front of the vase – the centrepiece of the suite – that he bequeathed to Greenwich Hospital. In the background is his Gothic-revival home, Kempton Park.**

Designs for furniture reflecting the national obsession with Nelson and maritime prowess appeared in Sheraton's *Cabinet Dictionary* as early as 1803. But despite the wealth of original documentation that has survived about the furniture and the lamp, no reference to the maker of the furniture has yet been discovered, and so his identity and the link with the maker of the lamp remain the subject of continuing speculation.

The furniture was originally upholstered in white watered Italian silk trimmed with "tabby and gold twist cord"; the striped green fabric with which it is now covered is a later replacement. Most of the furniture survives in largely unaltered condition, although the evidence of contemporary descriptions suggests that dramatic changes have been made to the couch. It was described on its arrival at Greenwich in 1815 as a "most superbly finished throne" with "a canopy head, burnished gold cornice and numerous masterly designs; the whole hung in rich drapery bordered with costly gold lace with silk fringe tassels".

Powerful decoration reinforces the theme of the heroism of Nelson, and the decorative heart of the suite is the intricately painted glass lamp, which shows the Battle of Trafalgar on one side and the Apotheosis of Nelson on the other. The dolphins not only refer to the Fish family name (a similar fish occurs on the family crest), but also symbolize maritime power. The lotus

bloom which fills the centre of the couch and appears on the lamp was believed to have been worshipped on the banks of the Nile; it is a reference to Nelson's victory at the Battle of the Nile, as are the crocodiles and sphinxes on the lamp. The laurel wreaths that frame the polescreens and the cornucopias that form the legs of the armchairs are classical motifs associated with heroism and plenty. The lamp also features oak leaves – the badge of the Royal Navy – and anthemion or honeysuckle, a flower associated with the decoration of ancient sarcophagi.

John Fish was the owner of Kempton Park, an impressive mansion in Surrey. He had inherited a fortune of nearly £500,000 from a relative whose money had been made manufacturing gunpowder, an essential commodity during the Napoleonic Wars. A generous philanthropist and patron of the arts, Fish was described as endowed with a "liberal spirit" and a "generous disposition". He married twice but had no children of his own. His first wife died in childbirth and he took a nephew under his

wing, paying for his "lamentably neglected" education and making him chief beneficiary of his estate. Many worthy causes were helped by loans from Fish, usually with little or no security, and after his death much of his fortune was lost to debtors.

Artistic patronage seems also to have preoccupied Mr Fish. He filled Kempton Park with lavish furniture and glass so spectacular that it inspired an article on glass staining in the British press in 1811. The lamp was described as "a vase of workmanship equally superb ... It is supported on a stand by three dolphins in carved wood, richly gilt, and represents in transparency the Battle of Trafalgar ..." Fish was so proud of it that a contemporary engraving shows him standing beside it, with his mansion, set in a deer-filled park, beyond.

The lamp was designed and made by William Collins, a glass manufacturer of 227 Strand, who numbered among his illustrious patrons the Duke of Sussex and Princess Elizabeth (a daughter of George III). Collins evidently specialized in "the

art of glass staining" and supplied Mr Fish with a window that was similarly decorated and a chandelier costing £700 for Kempton Park. The chandelier was also donated to Greenwich Hospital but appears to have become separated from the rest of the bequest and its present whereabouts are unknown. After Fish's death the lamp was returned to Collins, who engraved it with the inscription: "To the memory of Lord Viscount Nelson. The gift of the late John Fish, Esq. of Kempton Park. Presented by his widow and executrix, A.D. 1813." Having engraved it, Collins took it by horse and cart to Greenwich and installed it in the Painted Hall, for which services Mrs Fish was charged £31 17s (including an outstanding sum, perhaps because Mr Fish had neglected to fully pay for his treasured lamp).

At Greenwich the lamp continued to attract attention. An article in the *National Register* in 1813 described it in detail, ascribing the bequest to the fact that Mr Fish (in common with much of the British population) had been "animated with a deep

and lively sense of gratefulness and admiration for the eminent services of the hero of the Nile and Trafalgar". Meanwhile the furniture was still in need of a permanent home. In 1814, Chelsea Hospital was approached as a possible recipient, but declined the offer after inspecting it, because the lavish white and gold upholstery was considered inappropriate for a state-room where all the other furniture was a suitably regal crimson – and there was nowhere else for it to go. Greenwich Hospital was less fastidious and by 1815 the chandelier had been placed in the Council Room, and the rest in the Painted Hall, pending the return of Governor Hood from Bath, when it would possibly be moved to his drawing room.

Nearly six decades later the Hospital closed and was taken over by the Admiralty as a naval college. The furniture, including the lamp, was moved to Admiralty House. Here, in the official residence of the First Lord of the Admiralty, it was much admired, being affectionately known as "the Fish", and it remained there for the next century with few interruptions.

In the 1960s the office of the First Lord was abolished and the Prime Minister occupied Admiralty House during renovation of 10 Downing Street. An official report of the period stated that the furniture was in a fragile state, having been sat upon by the "families of British Empire Medal recipients during Investitures in Admiralty House when children's fingers had made explor-ations in the upholstery". The suite was therefore lent to Brighton Pavilion, where it can be seen surrounded by Regency splendour in which Mr Fish would have felt quite at home.

Far left **The extraordinary lamp made by William Collins reveals Regency design at its most imaginative. The Battle of Trafalgar is engraved on the glass vase at the top, and the sphinxes and crocodiles allude to Nelson's triumph in the Battle of the Nile.**

Left **The giltwood polescreens are formed as laurel wreaths – another reference to Nelson's heroism. A *mélange* of fish and classical and Egyptian motifs decorates the armchairs.**

49

Left Like the other upholstered pieces, the elegant window seats were made from carved and gilded wood. The front legs, which were made in the form of cornucopias (horns of plenty), are of a fashionable shape that was derived from French furniture designs.

Above The couch, the largest and most spectacular piece, may well have been altered, since it was described in 1815 as having "a canopy head, burnished gold cornice … the whole hung in rich drapery bordered with costly gold lace with silk fringe tassels".

Oak Half-tester Bed

Above **The design for the panelled head and half-tester was tailored to suit the evocative Gothic surroundings. We decided that a half-tester design rather than a full-tester was the right choice for this room since its open-raftered ceiling demanded a piece of considerable height.**

There can be few bedrooms more romantic than this one, with its sumptuous half-tester bed in superbly evocative Gothic surroundings. Nestling in the Somerset hills, the 12th-century priory in which this magnificent bed stands is a rare survivor of the dissolution of the monasteries, but the brief to design and make a bed to complement this medieval setting was not as straightforward as it first sounded.

The house, built from honey-coloured local stone, retains many of its original architectural features, including its cloisters, and is of unique historical importance. However, when the present owner bought the property parts of it had fallen into disrepair. So, with English Heritage looking over his shoulder, he began the long, painstaking task of sympathetically restoring and transforming it into an imaginative and unusual home. The architectural importance of the building placed enormous restrictions on how rooms could be changed and modernized, and therefore how furniture could be fitted into them.

The owner has a great knowledge of the theatre and his approach to the bedroom that he wanted to create was similar to the way he would have developed a stage set. He knew from the start that he did not want anything too fussy. But neither did he want an overly simple or "modern" bed because that would also look wrong. It may seem that such an elaborate bed is inappropriate as a furnishing for what was once a religious establishment, but, according to Chaucer, the residents of monasteries in the Middle Ages enjoyed a very comfortable lifestyle. His immortal monk, finely dressed in fur-trimmed robes and not overtroubled by the strict ordinances of the past, 'liked a fat swan best, and roasted whole'.

The bedroom is vast, with a high, open-raftered ceiling that looks like the upturned hull of a boat. Dominating the room at the far end is a huge Gothic window. The bed had to match up to its vivid Gothic setting, and be dynamic enough not to be swamped by the scale of the room.

Gothic architecture has spawned numerous revivals and supplied cabinet-makers with ideas over the centuries, but we

Above **It was this photograph of a 16th-century bed, with its striking carved chevron posts, that provided the inspiration for our design.**

decided to draw our inspiration from much earlier styles, when beds were regarded as among the most important furniture in a grand house. The few surviving beds that date back to the Renaissance show that large houses furnished their state bed-chambers with beds that were invariably lavishly carved and sumptuously upholstered. The intention was to impress visitors, although the draperies also performed an important function in protecting their occupant from piercing draughts and, in the days when numerous attendants in the bedchamber were the norm, in affording some privacy. Carving was the usual way to decorate early beds. Many had panelled heads adorned with very elaborate geometric, heraldic, or narrative designs, and the posts were similarly complex in form and decoration.

In these days of efficient central heating, draperies are no longer fundamental to the design of such a bed, but we decided that strong carving would provide the Gothic flavour we sought. We chose English oak as the main timber because this was the wood traditionally used for most good-quality furniture until the end of the 17th century, and its golden colour would give an injection of warmth to the room and work with the natural tones of stone, wooden rafters, and lime-washed walls. In the interest of overall harmony the finish was also left as natural as possible and we simply oiled the wood to emphasize its natural hue.

The top of the half-tester was designed to sit between two stone corbels, decorated with angels, that support the rafters. In Ralph Edwards's *Dictionary of English Furniture* we found a photograph of a 16th-century bed carved with distinctive chevron-patterned posts that we felt would create a suitably strong frame to stand between the corbels on each edge of the panelled back. The remaining decoration reflects the architecture of the room. The panelling, frieze, and bed posts were decorated with a trefoil-arched design that we took from the tracery of the window, while the ribbed ceiling of the half-tester echoes the ceiling beams, and turned pendants at each end mirror the downward thrust of the stone corbels.

Throughout the centuries all commissioned furniture has been tailored to suit both its surroundings and its patron. Seen in its magnificent setting, this bed provides a focal point in what could easily become overwhelmingly grand surroundings; while the powerful solidity of its design gives it a dramatic impact that seems particularly relevant to its owner's illustrious career.

51

Left **The bed's dynamic design creates a forceful focal point in the vast room. The oiled English oak from which it is carved already has a mellow richness, and this will intensify as the piece ages.**

Extraordinary Design

furniture of exemplary style

Whether it reflects a prevailing fascination with the East, an interest in classical antiquity, or profound religious or aesthetic conviction, the style of furniture has always been governed to a significant extent by the interests, beliefs, and way of life of its patrons and makers. Pieces displaying exceptional design may be the landmark creations of trailblazing designers or the masterpieces of craftsmen who, from a hotchpotch of sources and ideas, succeeded in creating furniture of outstanding appearance and form.

Left **The interior of this fascinating cylindrical secretaire is like a miniature classical temple. The desk was made in 1814 by one of Vienna's leading cabinet-makers, Johan Härle, from mahogany, maple, and ebonized wood, and may be the one that he made to qualify as a master craftsman.**

Japanned
Boston Highboy

This richly decorated japanned highboy still looks exotic today, so when it was first installed it must have brought a splash of oriental splendour to the interior it furnished. Despite the weeping willow trees and pagoda-like buildings that adorn the top, it comes from neither China nor Japan, but Boston, where it was among the most distinctive pieces of furniture made in the second quarter of the 18th century. The Chinoiserie decoration reveals the taste for oriental exoticism – one of the passions of furniture makers of this period.

Above **The highboy is appropriately displayed in a sitting-room furnished with other pieces of furniture of the Queen Anne period, at Bayou Bend, Houston.**

The technique of japanning was first described in a book published in England in 1688 by John Stalker and George Parker entitled *A Treatise of Japanning and Varnishing*. This influential book also contained engravings of pseudo-oriental patterns, including birds, flowers, figures, and pagodas, which were probably borrowed from examples of oriental lacquer and illustrated travel books. The book, which provided the inspiration for much Western japanning of the late 17th and 18th centuries, described in detail how the best effects could be achieved, suggesting suitable colours for the background and stressing the importance of finish, which, it said, should be polished until it "glisten and reflects your face like a mirror".

The Western fashion for japanned furniture was fuelled by the trickle of rare and expensive items of oriental lacquer that reached Europe from the Far East in the 17th century. Every owner of a grand and fashionable house longed for lacquer and there was never enough to satisfy the demand. Making oriental lacquer was a long and painstaking process in which a prepared wooden ground was coated with layers of resin made from the sap of the *Rhus vernicifera* tree. Each layer had to dry and harden before the next could be applied, and sometimes as many as twenty layers were used to achieve the distinctive lustrous surface, which was then decorated in a variety of ways.

The craze for lacquer led European craftsmen to devise a far less laborious way to imitate the effect. Western "japanning" (imitation lacquer) was achieved by covering the wood, usually

Above **The elaborate raised decoration and tortoiseshell background make this the most refined type of japanning executed in America in the 18th century. Earlier japanning was characterized by the use of a solid background colour; the mottled effect seen here was a later development.**

oak, with a layer of gesso (plaster) and coating it with layers of coloured varnish that could then be painted and gilded in pseudo-oriental style. The art became popular throughout Europe and infiltrated America with the immigrant craftsmen who settled in the flourishing centres of furniture making.

Boston was America's leading centre of japanning and its craftsmen developed their own idiosyncratic way to simulate the appearance of lacquer. Instead of covering oak with a layer of gesso, they favoured maple or pine, which were less porous and therefore did not need to be sealed with a layer of gesso. The background colour was then applied directly to the wood. (For this piece a streaked combination of crimson and black was used to give the effect of tortoiseshell, creating an American style quite unlike any European japanning.) Once coloured, the surface was coated with resin, before more painted decoration was added. Relief detail was applied with cast gesso or putty figures that were then decorated with paint and silver and gold powder and leaf.

The basic design of a highboy is simple: a chest raised on a stand with another chest of drawers above. However, in this case the basic form is refined in several ways. The lower part, consisting of two shallow and three deep drawers, is enlivened with a richly carved and gilded shell. The upper part, with four wide and two narrow drawers, has a small cupboard embellished with a lavishly carved and gilded shell in the centre. The heavy bonnet top, broken pediment, and vase finials all add architectural impact to the overall effect.

Japanned highboys were among the most opulent and stylish pieces of furniture made in America in the generally restrained Queen Anne period. Highboys had been made in England in the 17th century, but their popularity was short-lived. In America they stayed in vogue for much longer, becoming increasingly elaborate and developing distinctive characteristics according to when and where they were made.

So far only seven Boston japanned highboys have been discovered. This example, at Bayou Bend, Houston, Texas, was acquired by Ima Hogg (*see* page 65) from a New York dealer and is still in excellent condition. The master craftsman who made it remains unidentified, although experts have wondered whether he might be Thomas Johnston (1708–67), a famous japanner in Boston whose business card featured cherubs rather like the ones decorating the spandrels of this piece.

Right **The highboy at Bayou Bend has survived in remarkable original condition, although the finials and pendant drops are later replacements. Numerous craftsmen specializing in various disciplines would have been engaged for the creation of the piece – among them joiners, carvers, gilders, turners, and japanners.**

55

Chinoiserie Bed by William and John Linnell

Widely regarded as being among the most exciting Western furniture ever made, in the period when it was produced this outlandish "Chinese" bed must have appeared drastically different from mainstream furniture. Part of a suite of furniture made c.1754 for the 4th Duke of Beaufort, for Badminton House, it was to be the focal point in one of the first rooms to be entirely designed in "Chinese" style.

Right **The Chinese bed probably made by William and John Linnell is shown here as it looks today. Remarkably, the original lacquer surface of the bed has remained perfectly intact, although the yellow hangings which now adorn the bed are replacements for the original silk.**

Above **The evocative snarling dragon which decorates the pagoda roof of William and John Linnell's bed is made from carved and gilded wood and reveals their imaginative approach to the bedroom's Chinese theme.**

56

Right **Numerous designs for lavishly decorated beds, some in the Chinese taste, appeared in Thomas Chippendale's *The Gentleman and Cabinet-Maker's Director* in 1755. The design shown top left has many features in common with the Badminton bed.**

Charles Noel, 4th Duke of Beaufort, was the brother of Henry, the 3rd Duke, who had commissioned the outstanding Badminton Cabinet (*see* pages 32–5), and he proved to be as inspired a patron of contemporary furniture makers as his short-lived brother. His bedroom at Badminton anticipated the craze for rooms in the Chinese style, which became such a fashionable feature of grand houses that the 18th-century diarist Mrs Montague wrote with disapproval of how "sick of Grecian elegance and symmetry or Gothic grandeur and magnificence we must all seek the barbarous gaudy gout of the Chinese". Sadly the 4th Duke was not to enjoy his Chinese bedchamber for long, for he died in 1756 at the age of forty-seven, only two years after his extravagant room was complete.

The bed's design relates closely to Thomas Chippendale patterns which appeared in *The Gentleman and Cabinetmaker's Director* in 1755, although it was probably already made by the time this influential book was published. In 1754, when Dr Richard Pococke visited Badminton, he recalled a room "finished and furnished very elegantly in the Chinese manner". The bed is thought to be by William Linnell (1708–63) and his son John (1729–96) (*see* pages 60–1).

The Linnells were one of the century's foremost firms of cabinet-makers, and operated from premises in Berkeley Square, London. A surviving drawing for a "Chinese" chair by John Linnell has a fretwork back that is identical to the fretwork on the bedhead, and tasselled fringing very similar to the carved fringe surrounding the canopy of the bed. The Badminton suite included, along with the bed, eight chairs, standing shelves, a commode, and perhaps several pieces of writing furniture.

The walls were papered in Chinese paper and the windows and bed draped in sumptuous curtains and hangings – all probably supplied by the Linnells. The cost to the fashion-leading 4th Duke was the considerable sum of £800.

The Linnells, like many cabinet-makers of the period, were far more than mere furniture makers. They were able to offer their illustrious clients a comprehensive service that included interior design, spring cleaning, curtain-making, and supplying bedding; they even arranged funerals. Their particular strength as furniture makers lay in the quality of both their designs and their carved decoration.

The bed is typical of their imaginative approach: a fantastic confection of what an 18th-century cabinet-maker thought of as "Chinese". The head is made from a lattice of Chinese fretwork panels. The pagoda canopy, which is perhaps derived from illustrations of oriental buildings, is garnished with fronds of luxuriant foliage and crowned by an exotic cluster of spiky gilt-metal leaves, fenced by a fretwork gallery. At each corner, beautifully carved winged dragons with serpent-like bodies take flight, and the exotic effect is completed by the black, red, and gold japanning with which all the woodwork is embellished.

Above **This design for a "Chinese" chair by John Linnell also relates closely to the style of the bed. The fretwork back** is identical to the design of the bedhead, and the bed also incorporates the pagoda cresting and the fringed trim.

Giltwood Sofas by William and John Linnell

"I always thought it needed a warm sun to bring its frozen beauties to life ..." said the Marquess of Curzon's wife of the family's elegant residence, Kedleston Hall, in Derbyshire. But Kedleston's classical exterior belies the exuberance of the furniture within. In the drawing-room, four massive giltwood sofas have frames swathed with dolphins, writhing tritons, mermaids, and mermen, and draped with garlands of laurel. Made in 1765, they are among the grandest, most luxuriantly carved pieces of furniture made by William and John Linnell.

Above **This watercolour sketch, dating from 1761–2, shows John Linnell's design for the lavishly coloured mermaid and merman supports on the larger of the two pairs of sofas at Kedleston. It is one of several drawings that he made for this pair of sofas.**

Right **The blue damask upholstery and wall hangings in the grand Drawing Room are modern replacements but similar to those originally used. The alabaster columns framing the door came from the family's Derbyshire quarry.**

The inspiration for the sofas' imaginative design was to a large extent provided by the owner of Kedleston, Nathaniel Curzon, 1st Lord Scarsdale. One of the Linnells' most powerful patrons, Curzon was a connoisseur who possessed discerning taste and a substantial fortune. The design of these pieces reflects his dual passions: classical antiquity and the sea. Curzon's interest in classical art and architecture had been fuelled by the Grand Tour and by the numerous Italian works of art he acquired. His fascination with ships was in large part kindled by England's maritime success against the French, and several models, including one of Nelson's flagship HMS *Victory*, were later prominently displayed in the house.

Before he inherited the baronetcy and Kedleston in 1758, Curzon had already begun to formulate detailed plans for the reconstruction of the family home. As soon as he assumed the title he set about rebuilding the house in the Palladian style, engaging for the purpose several leading architects before finally entrusting Robert Adam with the interior decoration of the rooms. The state drawing-room in which the sofas stand is in the central section of the house, which contains all the formal reception rooms. An imposing room that was unmistakably designed to impress, it possessed a huge Venetian window that punctuated one wall, four richly decorated door-cases framed with alabaster columns, Corinthian capitals and pediments, and a ceiling, designed by Robert Adam, studded with motifs drawn from classical antiquity.

Right **One of the smaller pair of sofas has a back medallion filled with a profile portrait of Iris, the handmaiden of Juno, who features in its counterpart. The use of two pairs of sofas rather than a suite of chairs increases the monumental grandeur of the room.**

In such grandiose surroundings scale was important, and the sofas are appropriately huge: the larger pair measure 13ft (4m) in length and the smaller pair 12ft (3.7m). The executant architect, Samuel Wyatt, having seen the first sofa unwrapped and put in position, described his initial impression to Lord Scarsdale: "The gilding is by far the best done of any I ever saw, [and] it suits the place in point of size well."

Each of the carved figures that adorn the sofas reinforces the maritime theme. Their contorted poses call to mind the sumptuousness of baroque sculpture or furniture such as the Corradini throne seat (*see* pages 30-1), and presage the marine extravagance of the Regency Dolphin Suite (*see* pages 46–7). It is only in the serene classical profiles that punctuate the backs that there is a hint of the controlled neoclassical style with which Robert Adam is usually associated (*see* pages 100–1, the Venus and Diana Commodes).

By the time these sofas were made, William Linnell was reaching the end of his career (he died in 1763, two years before they were finished) and it seems likely that the responsibility for the design and creation of these remarkable pieces was largely due to his son, working in close collaboration with Robert Adam. The extent of Adam's influence on the finished sofas' design remains the subject of continuing speculation. An Adam drawing, dated 1762, of a more restrained sofa possessing classical caryatid end supports, and inscribed with the name of Lord Scarsdale, is in existence, a fact that strongly suggests that the architect did have a hand in the design. (This design was later used for a pair of sofas made for another of Adam's patrons, Mrs Montagu.)

John Linnell's designs for the sofas still exist and show that the central medallions decorating the backs of the larger pair were originally intended to contain the Scarsdale coat of arms instead of the classical heads. The supports on the two pairs of sofas are slightly different: the larger ones are carved as a merman with a conch and a mermaid with a lyre, emerging from bulrushes, while the smaller ones show a triton and a sea nymph. Both pairs of sofas have central supports in the form of dolphins entwined with bulrushes.

Installed in the drawing-room in 1765, these flamboyant pieces of furniture aroused huge interest, but received a mixed reception among contemporary arbiters of taste. The Duchess of Northumberland described them as "supported at the angles by large gilt figures which terminate in foliage". The splendid effect failed to enthrall her: "tho' very magnificent I think these frames rather too heavy," she wrote. The most colourful of the criticisms was that levelled by Horace Walpole, who saw in the sofas echoes of an earlier Linnell design. Two years before he began work on them, Linnell had created a design for George III's coronation coach. The design that was used for the coach was conceived by Sir William Chambers, but the alternative design produced by Linnell was lavishly adorned with tritons, mermaids, and palm fronds – all motifs that were resurrected in his drawings for the Scarsdale sofas.

It is no wonder then that Walpole, after a visit to Kedleston in 1768, famously recorded his impression of the Linnell sofas as: "settees supported by gilt fishes and sea gods absurdly like the King's coach".

The Craven
Urns

Deceptively, these sumptuously decorated urns look as if they were made from well-patinated bronze. The fact that wood – here, rich mahogany – can look so remarkably like sculpted metal is due not only to superbly fluid carving but also to the urns' design, which is loosely based on a pattern for a rococo silver urn published by the furniture designer John Linnell (see pages 56–9).

Above **A view of the Great Dining Room at Combe Abbey in 1909 shows the Craven urns flanking a side table at the far end of the room.**

The urns are thought to have been made for the London home of Fulwar, the 4th Baron Craven, in the 1760s. Baron Craven had a penchant for top-quality furniture and acquired many notable pieces for his residence, including a desk closely based on a Thomas Chippendale design and a canopy bed similar to a design by the architect James Paine. But the identity of the maker of these urns remains a mystery. When they were made leading designers were beginning to fall under the spell of classical taste. Robert Adam was a leading exponent of this neoclassical style, and bringing classical pedestals and urns into the dining-room is thought to have been his idea.

Pedestals and urns were designed to stand on either side of a sideboard or side table, where their elegant forms created an effective vertical emphasis which complemented the long, horizontal surface in the centre. This combination was found to be aesthetically extremely pleasing to the refined 18th-century arbiters of taste and soon such pieces became an intrinsic part of the décor of every fashionable dining-room.

As with most pedestals and urns, both top and lower part are made from the same wood, which in turn reflects the wood used for the central sideboard. Mahogany, which has been used here, was the favoured wood for most early examples, but later in the century furniture makers became increasingly adventurous in the shapes they used and in the methods of decoration they incorporated. Nearly all urns draw heavily on classical antiquity for their inspiration. A pair designed by Robert Adam for Saltram were painted to simulate ancient Greek vases.

The Craven urns are especially interesting because they bridge the gap between rococo extravagance and neoclassical

Left **The shape and fluted bodies of the urns are based on ancient sarcophagi and reflect the burgeoning neo-classical style of the time.**

Right **The urns are a *tour de force* of 18th-century carving. Their maker has incorporated a wealth of movement into crisply carved details such as the pine-cone finial, the goat heads, and the scrolled foliate supports on which they stand.**

restraint. Classical motifs predominate: the shape of the urns is based on ancient sarcophagi and the goats' heads allude to the Bacchic revelry that frequently appeared in dining-room furnishing, decorating plinths and terms (pedestals for sculptures). But here the goats are not carved as sculpted masks – the usual approach in neoclassical decoration – but in an extremely naturalistic way as if they were modelled from real goats.

In style the urns are far more elaborate than the bases on which they stand, perhaps because their design was inspired by contemporary designs for extravagantly ornamented silver urns, which would have adorned the sideboards of most affluent households of the day. One of the most likely sources for the design was an engraving published in 1760 by John Linnell in *A New Book of Ornaments useful for Silver-Smiths etc,* which had similar masks (although in this case they were lions) linked by swags of drapery.

Apart from bringing a generous helping of classical elegance to the dining room, urns and pedestals also fulfilled a practical function. When kitchens and dining rooms were often a long way apart, and when dining on a lavish scale was the fashion in grand houses, they were in many cases fitted out to be used during the meal.

The Craven urns are lead-lined and have gilt-metal taps, probably for iced water for drinking and so that servants could rinse cutlery and glasses during the meal. One of the pedestals is fitted with a metal-lined cupboard for warming plates (a heater in a metal container would have been placed at the base of the cupboard). The other has a metal drawer at the top that was possibly for holding the residual water after the rinsing of cutlery. Below is a deep drawer that would probably have been used for storing a chamber pot, since it was a common practice during lengthy 18th-century banquets for gentlemen to use this facility in the dining-room, rather than troubling themselves to leave the assembled party.

Although few details are known about the 4th Baron Craven, for whom the urns were originally made, the history of his remarkable urns has remained linked to that of his family for almost two centuries. Craven House in Drury Lane, London, the family home which had been built in the 1680s for the 1st Lord Craven, was demolished in 1805, and the Olympic Theatre was erected on the site. The goat urns, along with other furniture, were moved to the family's country residence, Combe Abbey, Warwickshire. Here they remained until the 1960s, when they were bought by Jeremy Cotton, owner of Tythrop Park. Recently they appeared on the market once again and were bought by another private collector.

61

The Duke of Atholl's
Medal Cabinet

A classical temple provides a wonderfully novel home for the medals and coins of an acquisitive 18th-century collector, but this cabinet is doubly intriguing because it is veneered in broom, a wood that is hardly ever used to decorate furniture. Why was such an odd choice made for such a prestigious piece? The answer lies in the family history of James, the 3rd Duke of Atholl, for whom the cabinet was made. The emblem of Atholl's family, the Murrays, was the broom flower, so when furniture was required for the ancestral home, Blair Castle, the use of broomwood veneer must have seemed extremely apt, if a little out of the ordinary.

Above **Blair Castle, in the Scottish Highlands, the ancestral home of the Earls and Dukes of Atholl. A castle has stood on the site for over 700 years, but the present building was extensively rebuilt in the mid-18th century after being besieged by Jacobite forces under the command of Lord George Murray.**

Right **This portrait of the keen medal and coin collector John Murray, later the 3rd Duke of Atholl, was painted by Thomas Bardwell in 1753, the year in which the Duke married his cousin, Lady Charlotte Murray.**

Among several pieces of furniture made in broomwood for Blair Castle are a bureau bookcase produced in 1758; and a pole-screen, a pair of card tables, and this remarkable cabinet, commissioned soon after, c.1765. All are thought to be the work of a local cabinet-maker, George Sandeman (1724–1803), of whom little is known except that, after he had served his apprenticeship in Scotland, he settled in London, where the work of leading cabinet-makers of the time, such as Thomas Chippendale, must have fired him with enthusiasm and ideas. On his return to his native Perthshire he was commissioned by John Murray, later the 3rd Duke of Atholl, to make the bureau bookcase, which includes the novel feature of a concealed compartment for medals and coins. Perhaps the Duke's collection outgrew this limited space and this is why he commissioned a grander, free-standing cabinet for them.

Although it is not known whether the Duke ever visited Italy, coins were popular souvenirs of the Grand Tour, and the design Sandeman chose was ideally suited to an 18th-century connoisseur of classical history and antiquities. A miniaturized version of one of the most famous monuments in Rome, the Temple of Septimius Severus, the cabinet façade is exquisitely decorated with miniature Ionic columns and topped with three miniature ivory statues that were possibly taken from a piece of

Renaissance furniture. The façade pulls forward on runners to reveal an interior containing banks of baize-lined mahogany drawers to store the precious objects.

The use of broomwood must have posed some practical problems for Sandeman since it is available only in very narrow strips. But he certainly made the most of this boldly grained wood and created a stunning stripy effect perfectly suited to the inventive design.

John, the 3rd Duke of Atholl (1729–74) had a family history almost as unusual as the cabinet that he commissioned. The son of the famous General Lord George Murray, he was the nephew rather than the son of the 2nd Duke. His uncle had two daughters, Jean and Charlotte, but no sons to inherit the title, so the family arranged that John would marry one of his cousins in order to keep the estate within the family. Jean, the eldest daughter, had other ideas: she eloped with Lord Crawford in 1747, but died a few months later. John turned his attentions to Charlotte, whom he married in 1753. The marriage seems to have been successful, producing six children, among them Lord George Murray, the inventor of a semaphore system later adopted by the Admiralty.

A keen patron of the arts, the 3rd Duke added greatly to the family's collection of furniture and paintings. From the portraitist Johann Zoffany he commissioned an outstanding family portrait of himself with his wife and six children, and he made major improvements to the grounds of Blair Castle and to the land around another, more intimate family home at Dunkeld that was later demolished. He laid out walks on the nearby Craig y Barns, naming the Grotto, in a sign of affection for his wife, Charlotte's Cave. He must have been fond of the dramatic highlands in which he lived, for he commissioned a local artist, Charles Stewart, to paint local scenes to decorate the dining room at Blair, at a time when landscape was rarely the subject of "serious" painting and more usually relegated to filling in the background.

Family records show that the Duke added to his coin collection throughout the 1750s and 1760s and made frequent and sometimes substantial payments for new acquisitions. For example, in September 1758 he is recorded as having spent £0 18s 0d for "2 Scotch coyns".

In 1774 the Duke became ill at Dunkeld and, in a state of distress after mistakenly swallowing smelling salts, drowned in the nearby River Tay. So bereft was his widow that she never returned to the much-loved house. Since that tragic event the remarkable medal cabinet has remained at Blair Castle as a reminder of its erstwhile owner.

Left **The Temple of Septimius Severus, or Portico of Octavio, is one of the most impressive pieces of architecture in Rome's Forum. It was on this archetypal classical building that Sandeman based the design of the cabinet for the 3rd Duke of Atholl.**

Above **The broomwood veneers are used in various ways: a parquetry design decorates the portico, while the cabinet's flat sides are punctuated with low-relief Venetian windows.**

63

Block-fronted Desk Bookcase

A triumph of American furniture making, the block-fronted desk bookcase is an exceptionally innovative example of that country's colonial craftsmanship. Most 18th-century American furniture is obviously linked to European patterns, but this distinctive style was the invention of a unique group of makers working in Newport, Rhode Island, in the second half of the century. Fewer than a dozen of these remarkable desks survive, each with slight variations. The impressive open bonnet top on this example makes it a particular rarity.

Above **Bayou Bend was built by Ima Hogg in 1927, and donated to the Houston Museum of Fine Art in 1957. The house contains a unique collection of American domestic furniture.**

Instantly recognizable by its undulating surfaces and carved shells, block-fronted furniture was made in various forms. You may come across knee-hole desks, chests, highboys, and even clock cases in this pattern, but desk bookcases were the largest and most impressive pieces. This desk, at Bayou Bend, Houston, is a typically handsome and impressive example.

During the 18th century Newport was a thriving port and one of the major American centres of furniture making. Although the desk is not marked or labelled by a maker, its style links it to furniture made in this area by two renowned cabinet-making families: the Goddards and the Townsends. There were more than twenty furniture-making members of these two Quaker families. Several of the Goddards and Townsends inter-married, mingling their histories and fortunes, and for three generations they dominated the manufacture of Rhode Island furniture, earning a reputation for craftsmanship and design.

Like most block-fronted furniture, the desk bookcase is divided vertically into three sections. On the two outer thirds the raised "blocks" or panels bulge outwards and the shells above them are also carved in matching relief. The central section, however, bows inwards and the concave shell is carved into the surface of the wood. The visual effect of the alternating raised and recessed areas is to create a rippling contrast of light and shade across the surface of the piece.

This dramatic effect was a considerable achievement by the craftsmen, requiring a complex process of construction.

Above **The Drawing Room at Bayou Bend, where prime examples of 18th-century American furniture and heavy panelling together create an appropriate setting for the striking shell desk bookcase.**

The convex shells and panels were made separately and applied to the main carcass, while the concave areas were cut out from the solid wood.

Because the front of the bookcase desk has been divided into three, the basic bureau-bookcase design has been adapted in a variety of novel and interesting ways. You might expect the top section to open centrally, but in fact it opens between panels two and three on the right-hand side. The left-hand door is therefore twice as big as the one on the right, so that the join between the double-panelled door is hinged, presumably so that it would fold to create a balanced effect with the other door if the desk was left open. Behind the hinged doors the cupboard is also divided into three main sections which are in turn subdivided into a mass of smaller compartments and pigeon-holes. The tripartite theme continues as your eye moves down the desk. Instead of the usual central lock and escutcheon, there is one on each side. The desk opens downwards in the conventional way, revealing a space again divided into three, with three carved shell drawers set into arches interspersed with open compartments and small drawers.

Such striking pieces of furniture must always have been highly coveted and only affordable to the most successful and affluent buyers of the day. They were highly practical pieces, but their large size (this one is 99in/251cm tall and 42in/107cm wide) also made them eloquent symbols of wealth and status.

The principal wood used for the desk was Santa Domingo mahogany, a richly coloured wood of characteristically straight grain. Under its mahogany façade seven different woods have been identified as having been used, including eastern white pine, soft maple, chestnut, and red cedar. This extraordinary variety reflects the abundance of timbers that the 18th-century American furniture maker had readily to hand.

In many ways Ima Hogg, the creator of Bayou Bend, the house where this desk now takes pride of place, was every bit as exceptional as the furniture she bought. There cannot be many collectors, however keen, who begin buying as children and are still adding to their collection at the age of ninety. Ima Hogg's fortune was largely inherited from her father, who was Governor of the State of Texas and one of the first Texan oil millionaires. Ima built the elegant home at Bayou Bend in 1927, and in 1957 donated house and contents to the Houston Museum of Fine Arts, in order to provide a cultural link between Texas and the heritage of the rest of America, by displaying the best of the nation's art and artefacts.

When Ima bought the piece from a New York dealer in 1952, it was the first example of its kind to reach the open market for nearly thirty years. It stands today in the Drawing Room at Bayou Bend, a reminder both of Ima's discerning taste and the talented Rhode Island cabinet-makers of two centuries ago.

65

Left **Block-fronted furniture such as the Bayou Bend shell desk bookcase was unique to the Newport, Rhode Island, area, where it was made over a relatively lengthy period from 1760 to 1790.**

Baltimore Lady's Desk

66

Above **In the Baltimore Drawing Room at the Winterthur Museum, Delaware, the lady's desk (not visible here) is appropriately displayed surrounded by other examples of Baltimore furniture of the Federal period.**

Any elegant lady of the late 18th century would have been proud to have this lady's desk in her boudoir. She might have penned the occasional love letter at it, while checking on her make-up and coiffure whenever the fancy took her. Nutty yellow satinwood veneers contrasted with dark mahogany and interspersed with elegantly painted gold and black glass panels give the piece a strikingly elegant appearance. The combination of a clever design and tasteful decoration make this example one of the most sophisticated and unusual of a small group of desks that were produced in the flourishing town of Baltimore c.1795–1810.

Right **The desk's elegant shape, tapered legs, and the expensive timbers with which it is veneered are typical of the sophisticated furniture of the beginning of the 19th century in Baltimore. The painted panels above the legs are made from *verre églomisé* and, like the *klismos*, derived from Sheraton's pattern books.**

Far right **The lady's desk was based on this design by Sheraton for a lady's cabinet and writing table.**

In its overall shape the lady's desk is inspired by patterns for a "Lady's Cabinet and Writing Table" published by the influential English cabinet-maker Thomas Sheraton in the *Cabinet-Maker and Upholsterer's Drawing Book* in 1791–4. Sheraton's designs in turn were based on the French *bonheur du jour*. However, the cabinet-makers of Baltimore have made the piece very much their own by decorating it with painted glass (or *verre églomisé*, as it was known), a method of ornamentation in which they excelled. The desk's five painted panels decorated with gilded classical figures against a black background are all made from glass painted on the reverse. The central panel is especially interesting since it shows a figure reposing on a *klismos*, a form of antique Greek chair that was revived by the French cabinet-maker Georges Jacob in the late 1780s, and spread like wildfire on both sides of the Atlantic in the Empire period. This is one of the earliest illustrations of a *klismos* in America.

The cupboards on each side of the mirror conceal two drawers and pigeon-holes. Below, three joined panels can be raised to slide into the top and reveal more compartments and drawers. The writing surface below unfolds "like a card table", as Sheraton put it, and is supported by the long drawer below.

The craftsmen of Baltimore were highly skilful in their use of wood, and the veneers surrounding the oval central mirror are

Above **The central *verre églomisé* panel shows a Grecian figure reposing on a sabre-legged *klismos* chair.**

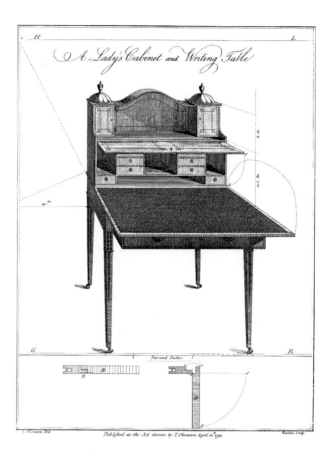

67

cut so that they radiate towards it, creating a dramatic central focus. Also, the veneers around the panels are mitred to draw the eye towards the figures. Ovals feature prominently in the overall design – the shape was highly fashionable at this period – and chair backs, tables, and many other pieces can be seen that reflect the form. Here the oval-shaped mirror is repeated in the five inset panels that decorate each of the five compartments in the upper part of the desk.

The black and gold of the panels is cleverly echoed by the golden satinwood and deep mahogany and ebony stringing and re-echoed in the painted domes each side of the mirror. Satinwood and mahogany were the most fashionable and expensive woods at this time and only used for the choicest pieces.

Baltimore was, around the turn of the century, a flourishing trading post rivalling other centres on the East Coast such as Philadelphia and New York. The city's population had more than doubled in a decade and an affluent growing market created a demand for top-quality furniture. Around 200 cabinet-makers are known to have been working in the area around this period. Little of their work was labelled and few pieces can be definitely ascribed to a particular maker. We still do not know who made this elegant desk or who commissioned it, but it certainly ranks among Baltimore's masterpieces.

Empress Josephine's Bed

Sumptuous yet exceptionally stylish, Empress Josephine's bed still stands in her glamorous circular bedchamber at Malmaison. Designed by the architect Berthault and made by Jacob-Desmalter, the leading cabinet-maker of the day, the bed encapsulates all the refinement and elegance of the furniture made in the Empire period. As the bed in which she died in 1814, it is also among the most intensely personal of the Empress's furnishings, a poignant reminder of the life of one of the most bewitching personalities of the time.

Above **The château of Malmaison was bought by Josephine at the end of the 18th century and transformed into a showpiece residence with the help of the leading architects Charles Percier and Pierre-François Léonard Fontaine. The elegant interiors were furnished in the distinctive style that prevailed throughout Napoleon's rule.**

Josephine acquired the château at Malmaison, in France, in 1799, while Napoleon was campaigning in Egypt, and it was to this, her favourite residence, that she withdrew after their divorce. Although Josephine extended and refurbished the château, it was by no means palatial, and both the interiors and furnishings she commissioned provide revealing glimpses of her personality and taste. Napoleon described Josephine as having "more grace and charm than anyone I have ever seen", and this description could equally be applied to the bedroom that his wife redecorated in 1812.

Most of the interiors at Malmaison had been designed and decorated by Napoleon's prized architects, Charles Percier and Pierre-François Léonard Fontaine, but the new bedroom scheme was the work of Berthault, one of Percier's students, who had already taken charge of the design of another of Napoleon's residences, the château of Compiègne. Berthault grew in Josephine's esteem largely as a result of his inspired landscaping of the gardens. Josephine was an enthusiastic plant collector, brought up in the West Indies and fascinated by exotic flora and trees. At Malmaison, aided by Berthault, she created gardens and conservatories filled with imported plants, trees and over 250 varieties of rose that became one of the most important collections of the day. Her passion for botany is also reflected in the styles of textiles used for upholstering furniture. She favoured light fabrics often featuring delicate floral motifs. Berthault's design looked like an extremely glamorous tent, with

Left **Josephine portrayed in her coronation robes by François Baron Gérard in 1807. Her spectacular costume was designed by the artist Jean-Baptiste Isabey.**

Right **The sumptuous swags of drapery decorating the bedchamber's walls and the bed itself reflect the fashion for tents that became a feature of many beds of the Empire period, partly in response to Napoleon's military prowess.**

Left **Empress Marie-Louise's beautifully decorated bedroom at the château de Compiègne was also designed by the architect Louis Berthault. The bed was one of the earliest and most lavish examples of the new antique style that became increasingly fashionable. Gilded angels holding back the bed's tented drapery highlight the royal occupant's status.**

walls draped in amaranth (deep crimson) muslin apparently supported by slender, gilded tent-post pillars.

During this period the appearance of beds changed dramatically. Instead of the traditional arrangement in which the head of the bed was placed against a wall, the Empire style favoured beds raised on a platform and set lengthways against a wall, so that the bed was primarily viewed from the side. Positioned in this way, Josephine's golden bed provided a striking focal point for the circular room. The design was not unprecedented, for it was partly inspired by a bed that Berthault had made for Empress Marie-Louise (Josephine's successor in Napoleon's affections) at Compiègne. However, the heavily carved gilt wood supports at the bed's head differ in that the cornucopias are crowned by seated swans, which were one of Josephine's favourite emblems.

The support at the foot of the bed, carved in the form of a cornucopia overflowing with fruit and flowers, mirrors the bold floral decoration on the side rail, which is pierced with a laurel wreath encircling the initial "J". This motif in turn reflects the design used to embroider the matching chairs commissioned with the bed. White hangings, made from muslin embroidered in golden thread, give a refreshing lightness to the overall design.

The bed itself has not always remained at Malmaison. When Josephine died it was inherited by her son, Prince Eugène, who, having married Auguste-Amelie of Bavaria, took it, together with the room's other contents, to Munich. For more than half a century it remained there, until, during renovation of the château in 1868, it was presented to Napoleon III and returned to its original setting.

The canopy presently above the bed is a replacement commissioned by Napoleon III at that time. There was no eagle in the original design, which featured flowers carved in a far less naturalistic manner in keeping with those on the base. Recently the wheel-like room has once again been restored to its original state and the bed at its gilded hub creates both a magnificent focal point and a potent symbol of the life of France's dazzling erstwhile Empress.

71

Left **The coronation of Napoleon and Josephine, which took place on 2 December 1804, was memorably orchestrated by the celebrated architects Percier and Fontaine. The coronation coach was drawn by eight light bays decked out in red Morocco harness.**

Above **A watercolour of the famous beauty Madame Recamier's bedroom shows the prevailing taste for beds positioned along a wall and softened by canopies of light fabric – usually muslin or silk. Designed by Berthault, the bed features swans, which were also used for Josephine's bed.**

Shaker Built-in Storage

These functional but subtly designed built-in cupboards epitomize the Shakers' unique and refreshingly clean-cut approach to furniture. But perhaps their most outstanding feature is their extraordinarily modern appearance. The pure forms adopted by Shaker furniture makers anticipate, with amazing accuracy, furniture design of the 20th century. Yet these cupboards were built more than a century and a half ago, in the 1830s, when flowery extravagance was the prevailing style for most furniture (see pages 108–9).

Above **Shouting, dancing, and shaking in religious ecstasy were an intrinsic part of the devotional ceremonies of the Shakers, who were also known as the Shaking Quakers.**

The Shakers were the most successful of the many religious groups that settled in America in the 19th century. A breakaway sect of the Quakers, the group took its name from its distinctive religious ceremonies, during which members would tremble ecstatically. The Shakers' spiritual leader was Mother Anne Lee, who brought the first followers to America, in 1774, to avoid religious persecution in England. Mother Anne Lee and the group's subsequent leaders established the rules to which every "believer" (member of a Shaker community) was required to adhere. The uncompromising way of life included being bound by a strict code of celibacy, not being allowed any personal possessions, sharing communal dwelling houses, and living apart from the rest of society. The communities were industrious and creative, and by the middle of the 19th century there were over 6000 believers living in twenty well-structured, self-sufficient villages.

The distinctive furniture made by the Shakers reflects their unusual lifestyle and beliefs. Each village was divided into groups of up to one hundred members, called families, who lived in specially designed dwelling houses. The Church family was the most important group in each village, and the built-in cupboard that fills the corner of the simply furnished room on the opposite page is one of several similar pieces made in 1830 for the Church family dwelling house at the Hancock Village, Massachusetts. Some ninety-four believers lived in the house, four or more sharing a retiring room such as this.

Above **The Church family laundry and machine shop at the Hancock Shaker Village, Massachusetts. The machine shop produced much of the furniture and many of the community's other artefacts.**

Mother Ann Lee had advocated that her followers "provide places for all your things, so that you may know where to find them at any time day or night". Furniture, like other material belongings, had to be shared. Cleanliness was a major consideration in the lives of Shakers. "There is no dirt in heaven," wrote Mother Ann Lee, and built-in furniture had the benefit of providing storage behind a façade which could not trap dust. The building and interior furnishing of the Hancock Church family house was masterminded by the village elder, William Deming, who wrote: "There are … 240 cupboard doors, 396 drawers … they take up little room and are not to be cleaned under."

Another example of the Shakers' passion for organization is the storage room shown overleaf. This was made for the Church family dwelling house in the Canterbury Shaker Village, New Hampshire, when the 18th-century dwellling house was extended. Beneath the two long, sloping eaves of the attic storey, six walk-in wardrobes, fourteen cupboards, and more than a hundred drawers were constructed. The metal numbers with which each storage compartment is tagged allowed each individual or family to identify their own space.

Attic storage rooms such as this were made to hold unseasonal clothes and other equipment, and the Shakers' capacity for regimentation extended to how and when such cupboards were used. Believers were not permitted to change from summer into winter clothes or vice versa at will; the day was decided by community elders and all believers followed their direction in changing both clothing and linen. The cupboards were then strewn with dried aromatic plants, bed linen stored in drawers and unseasonal clothes cleaned and carefully put away on hand-made hangers marked with the wearer's initials.

The simplicity of the cupboards also reflects the Shakers' deep-rooted dislike of superfluous decoration. Made primarily from pine which has been stained ochre and left unvarnished, they display no carving or elaborate mouldings, so that the surface and grain of the wood assumes paramount importance. Full-length doors are interspersed with blocks of half-length cupboards and drawers, giving a strong architectural feel. Simplicity and perfection are the overriding principles behind the design and the makers clearly never forgot Mother Ann Lee's advice to: "Do all your work as though you had a thousand years to live and as you should if you knew you must die tomorrow."

Right **The cupboards in the retiring room were typically made from readily available indigenous woods. In this case the cupboard doors are faced with stained butternut on a pine carcass.**

Overleaf **One of the most impressive examples of the Shakers' built-in cupboards, the attic storage room at the Canterbury Village shows their preference for simple designs with no superfluous decoration.**

Chairs by
Frank Lloyd Wright

These striking dining chairs would not appear out of place in an ultra-modern interior, and yet they were made less than a decade into the present century. They are outstanding examples of the radical furniture designs of Frank Lloyd Wright (1869–1959), who was a pioneer not only of modern architecture but also of furniture design. Like the minimalist Shaker creations of the previous century (see pages 72–5), these chairs foretold with extraordinary accuracy the route 20th-century furniture design was to follow.

Above **The Darwin D Martin House, in Buffalo, New York State, built in 1902–4, reveals Lloyd Wright's quest for an "organic architecture" in which form and function merged with their surroundings.**

Right **Frank Lloyd Wright photographed in Washington in 1955. His avant-garde architecture, theories, and furniture designs reappraised traditional forms and were to have a profound effect on 20th-century design.**

Right **Unlike most traditional dining chairs, the chairs used in the living area of the Martin House were designed to be seen from the back. Their unusual design, with their backs dropping to the floor, creates a visual wall that separates the open-plan dining area from the rest of the room.**

Lloyd Wright's furniture developed alongside his architectural designs. He is famed for completely rethinking the way in which space was organized in the traditional home. For him furniture was an integral part of the surrounding architecture, which in turn was integral to the environment in which it stood. He called this approach "organic architecture" and wrote of it: "it is quite impossible to consider buildings as one thing, its furnishing another and its setting and environment still another".

These chairs were made for Darwin D Martin's house, in Buffalo, New York State, in 1902–4. At the time it was built the Martin House was Lloyd Wright's most important residential commission to date, and comprised the house, a long pergola, a conservatory, a stable block, and a gardener's cottage. He was an admirer of the traditionally crafted, functional objects designed by the Arts and Crafts movement, and his furniture designs also reflect his interest in Japanese aesthetics and belief in the increasing importance of machines. Early chairs such as these were one-offs, but they were designed with machine production in mind – a significant step toward the approaching age of mass-production.

The tall-backed dining chair is related to one of Lloyd Wright's earliest chair designs, for his own house at Oak Park, Illinois. The design was tailored to the new "modern" dining areas found in many Lloyd Wright houses. Living spaces merged, gone was the separate dining room, in which the table was placed centrally and chairs, when they were not in use,

were lined against the walls, and with this went traditionally designed dining chairs, made to be seen from the front.

Lloyd Wright's chairs were designed to be stored against the table and to be viewed mainly from the back. He lent them visual interest by using back spindles that drop almost to the floor. There was no carved decoration; the shape of the chair and strong grain of the wood – here oak – were enough. The tall back created impact and limited the dining area in much the same way that walls did in more conventional houses.

The barrel chair, which was designed for the living area, was a deceptively simple design that was devised with both function and comfort in mind. The idea for an upright easy chair is loosely based on the bergère of previous centuries, but Lloyd Wright reinterpreted the form in a characteristically modern way. The sweeping curves of the back and arms might suggest the fluid shapes of art nouveau, but these have been simplified into abstract forms. The chair is heavy and fairly large, but because the designer has given it a smooth horseshoe base rather than legs, it can be dragged easily into place. The back and arms are precisely designed to support the occupant; the arms are upraised to provide a comfortable rest.

At the time they were made, these chairs must have seemed shockingly bizarre. But as we look at them today in the setting for which they were made, they are perfectly in tune with their surroundings. As Lloyd Wright put it: "the very chairs and tables ... are of the building itself, never fixtures upon it".

Above **The barrel chair created for the Martin House presages similar designs used later by Lloyd Wright. Deceptively simple in shape, the curving back and sculpted arms are designed to support the body.**

77

Manhattan
Screen

The Metropolitan Museum of Art, New York's Public Library, The Dakota Building, Brooklyn Bridge, the Empire State Building, and the Chrysler Building – this dramatic marquetry screen based on New York's familiar skyline gives you the city old and new at a glance. Designed by David Linley Furniture for the advertising agency Lowe International, who had recently opened a new office in Manhattan, the six-panelled screen had to make an immediate impact on visitors to the agency and be relevant to the surroundings.

Above **One of the preparatory drawings that were made to finalize the arrangement of buildings on the screen. The silhouettes of skyscrapers in the distance were dropped from the final design.**

Right **Completed in 1931, the Empire State Building took only two years to build. It has 102 storeys, and measures 1472ft (448.6m) from sidewalk to TV mast – the world's third tallest building. On a clear day the Empire State is visible from up to 80 miles (128km) away.**

New York seemed an obvious choice for the subject-matter but deciding which buildings to use and how to approach them was more tricky. While we were having a cup of hot chocolate with our client he described to us his favourite buildings and this provided the starting point for the commission. Before the final choice was made, we took numerous photographs of the contending buildings. Some shots were more difficult to get than others – stopping on Brooklyn Bridge to take a photo of the view is no joke in rush hour!

We chose these six structures to create a series of visual contrasts, and to give the realistic appearance of the jumbled heights and architectural styles that make up the Manhattan skyline. To achieve the required effect a degree of artistic licence was necessary. For example, you would never be able to see both the top of the Metropolitan Museum and the Empire State Building at the same level, and so in order to include our chosen façades scales were juggled, and some buildings were condensed while others were enlarged.

The buildings were also arranged to achieve the maximum visual impact. The Empire State Building and the Chrysler Building were positioned on either side of the centre to draw the eye into the middle and to increase depth. This miscellany of structures is tied together by the use of dyed blue sycamore, which provides the sky above and the river at the bottom.

Although in most cases our architectural screens show a minimum of light and shade, here, in order for the buildings to

Above **The East River, spanned by the graceful arch of Brooklyn Bridge, provides a horizontal counterbalance to the predominantly vertical emphasis of the screen. The darkness of the water echoes the night sky, forming a frame top and bottom for the juxtaposed buildings.**

Right **Six buildings of contrasting age and form were chosen to encapsulate the pot-pourri of Manhattan's skyline. The buildings of London, Paris, and Venice have been used on other screens to create a similar composite effect.**

"read" clearly, some shadow had to be incorporated. The less dramatic gradation of tone was created simply by alternating the direction of the wood grain.

In some situations (such as the tall, narrow buildings) more dramatic light and shade had to be shown. Here we used woods of deeper, richer tones on the side of the building in shadow (left-hand side). The sculptural elements – for example, the statues and heads decorating some of the buildings – were created by using a black and white photocopier to reduce the

photograph of a three-dimensional sculpture to a two-tone image that was composed entirely of light and shade. From this a template was made from which were cut the marquetry pieces depicting the statues.

Each of the dozen or more different woods that have been incorporated were chosen for their characteristic qualities. Among them are oak, vavona, madrone, harewood, sycamore, satinwood, elm, Swiss pear, macassar ebony, and box. For example, macassar ebony has distinctive brown flecks in a

black background. In this piece these flecks create the effect of windows on the Empire State Building.

No one as yet has hazarded a guess at how many pieces had to be painstakingly cut and fitted together to create the final jigsaw of woods, but a screen of this size (about 8ft/2.4m by 12ft/3.7m) and complexity takes a single craftsman some four months to make. As with most high-quality furniture, the piece owes its success to both an inspired design and the accuracy and skill of the draughtsmen and cabinet-makers who made it.

Extraordinary Craftsmanship

furniture of notable artistry and technical skill

Left and below **This intricately inlaid rosewood Indo-Portuguese credence table, used for celebrating mass, was probably made in Lahore, India, c.1610. Indian decorative style mingles with traditional Christian subject-matter in the detailed images created from minute slivers of ivory, ebony, and horn.**

The awe-inspiring technical skill that goes into making and embellishing fine furniture is fundamental to its appeal. Over the centuries techniques such as carving, turning, marquetry, gilding, lacquering, and casting metal mounts have evolved to enrich furniture both functional and decorative. At the same time cabinet-makers have long struggled with the limitations of the materials and tools available to them to produce furniture of exceptional accomplishment.

The Coronation Chair

One of the most ancient seats in Britain, the Coronation Chair was made at the command of Edward I c.1297–1300. Edward had captured the Stone of Scone from the Scots and wanted a throne to hold the sacred stone on which, throughout the centuries, Scottish kings had been seated for their coronation and on which Jacob was believed to have rested his head when he had his miraculous dream. Throughout its chequered history, and despite the ravages of time, the boys of Westminster School, and political activists, the Coronation Chair has remained a fascinating testimony to the durability of medieval craftsmanship.

Above **This painting, by an unidentified artist, of the Coronation of Queen Victoria in 1837, shows the monarch seated on the Coronation Chair, which traditionally has been draped with brocade.**

Right **In what is believed to be the earliest illustration of the Coronation Chair, a 13th-century illuminated manuscript shows the coronation of a king, possibly Edward II. The manuscript is kept at Corpus Christi, Cambridge.**

Right **The Coronation Chair now stands in the Chapel of St Edward the Confessor at Westminster Abbey. Most of the original finials and crockets and pierced Gothic frieze have disappeared, as has the painted decoration. The lion's feet were probably added in the 16th century.**

Edward commissioned his wooden throne from his painter, Master Walter of Durham. It was made in simple medieval style from solid planks of oak joined with wooden dowels, then carved and painted. The cost to the king was 100 shillings.

Apart from in times of war and 1657, when it was moved to Westminster Hall for Oliver Cromwell's inauguration as Lord Protector, the chair has remained in Westminster Abbey ever since its installation. Usually it resides, as it always has done, in the Chapel of St Edward the Confessor and only when it is being used for coronations and ceremonies such as royal jubilees is it moved to the centre of the Abbey.

The chair's pointed gables, crockets, pinnacles, and arcading are drawn straight from Gothic architecture; so much so that none of the decorative elements would look at all out of place carved from stone and attached to the surrounding stone walls. In its original state the chair looked very different from the way it does now. Around the Stone of Scone there was a Gothic quatrefoil grille decorated with painted shields that have since broken off. There was Gothic arcading on the inside of the chair, two carved leopards added to the decoration, and the piece was painted predominantly in white and gold.

A few decades after Master Walter had finished decorating his chair it was completely renovated in a far more sumptuous

manner. The interior arcading was erased and the piece was covered with lavish gilded and lustre decoration. An image of an enthroned king was painted on the back of the throne and around him an elaborate arrangement of animals, birds, fruit, and flowers was stamped into the gilding, producing a variety of richly textured images. In parts of the chair the decoration was further embellished by covering the wood with thin layers of tin. Translucent coloured varnishes were applied to these, followed by patterns painted in gold leaf and protected by a sheet of glass. The effect must have been spectacular.

Since then the chair has been modifed by a number of monarchs, usually in preparation for their coronation. Lion's feet were probably added in 1509, perhaps for the enthronement of Henry VIII, although the feet at the back may have been replaced in 1727, before George II's coronation. George IV had the lions regilded rather gaudily and removed the cresting at the gable's apex. In Queen Victoria's reign the cresting was crudely replaced – it was hammered to the back with long nails.

The reason for this lack of concern for the chair's condition is perhaps that for state occasions it was customarily covered with a lavish cloth, usually woven from silver or gold thread and held in place with nails. After the service spectators would surge forward to tear a piece of cloth from the throne as a memento of the event, leaving behind nothing but the nails. In consequence scores of nails or their scars have been left embedded in the wood. When the chair was X-rayed before the coronation of Elizabeth II in 1953 a buried scrapyard of metal was disclosed.

In the 19th century schoolboys and tourists would often inscribe their initials on the throne. Several names have been identified as past pupils of Westminster School, and one inscription on the seat reads: "P. Abbott slept in this chair 5–6 July 1800". Worse lay in store as the century progressed. In 1887, in preparation for Queen Victoria's jubilee, the chair was "restored" with a thick layer of brown varnish. Writing in the *Athenaeum*, one critic protested that it had been "vulgarised into the semblance of the hall chair of a Cockney Gothic villa".

Another close shave came in 1914, when suffragettes made a cocktail of nuts, bolts, and explosive, packed it in a bag and hung it on one of the pinnacles of the chair. The device exploded, causing considerable though not irreparable damage to the piece. During the First World War the chair and the Stone of Scone were moved to the Chapter House of the Crypt for safety. The threat of invasion was so real in the Second World War that the chair was sent to Gloucester Cathedral while the Stone was interred in a vault in Westminster Abbey.

The most recent dramatic episode in the Coronation Chair's venerable life came in 1950, when Scottish nationalists stole the Stone and took it to Arbroath Abbey. Fortunately, before long the relic was reunited with this remarkable chair.

83

The Nerli-Morelli Cassoni

The marriage in 1472 between Lorenzo di Matteo di Morelli and Vaggia di Tani di Francesco Nerli must have been a spectacular occasion. Like many affluent Florentines during the Renaissance, Morelli commissioned various pieces of furniture to celebrate the wedding, including this fine pair of cassoni for his home in Borgo Santa Croce. Decorated chests of this type were traditionally made to commemorate a marriage, and were sometimes paraded through the streets as part of the wedding procession.

Top **This detail of the front of the Morelli cassone shows part of the dramatic painting of Camillus Defeating the Gauls. The subject was taken from Livy's *Histories*.**

Above **On one of the side panels of the Nerli cassone is depicted a figure personifying Temperance, pouring wine from a gourd.**

Since Vaggia Nerli brought an ample dowry of 2000 florins her husband could well afford to buy elegant furnishings for the marital home. The cassoni he commissioned were elaborately carved with scrolls, acanthus moulding, and scales by a local craftsman, Zanobi di Domenico, and were typically brilliantly painted with colourful historical scenes by Jacopo di Sellaio and Biagio d'Antonio. A further, indispensable embellishment was the coats of arms of the Nerli and the Morelli families.

At that time marriage in wealthy families was largely a financial and political alliance in which sentiment tended to play a minor role. Objects made to mark such unions had to be unambiguously indicative of wealth and status. To a wealthy 15th-century Florentine a cassone was a symbol of prestige and power in much the same way that an ornate cabinet would have been to his 17th-century counterpart, or a mechanical roll-top desk would have been in the 18th century (*see* pages 126–7). Cassoni were intended to impress, which is why the Nerli-Morelli pieces are massive (83in x 76in x 30in/208cm x 193cm x 76cm), much bigger than a modern chest, and were decorated in the most eye-catching way available at the time: with paintings of colourful scenes, carving, and lavish gilding.

Apart from possessing stunning decoration, the Nerli-Morelli cassoni are exceptional because they are the only known examples to have retained their original *spalliere*, or rear panels. Many 15th-century cassoni originally had these, but because they were attached to the wall rather than the chest, in

Left **A side view of the Nerli cassone shows heavily carved corner scrolls that include the family's coat of arms. The carved lion's-paw feet are later additions – originally there was a solid plinth support.**

many cases they have become separated over the centuries. The *spalliere* on the chests shown here have at some stage been attached to the pieces themselves – an alteration that makes it imposible to fully open the lids.

These chests are made from poplar that was coated with gesso before being carved and painted. Florentine craftsmen of the time were dominated by all-powerful guilds who prevented them from encroaching on one another's specialty. Therefore several people were involved in the making of the Nerli-Morelli cassoni, which as a result represent a unique collaboration between the artists who painted the panels and the craftsman who created the exuberantly carved framework.

The paintings that decorate the *spalliere* and front panels illustrate historical scenes from Livy's *Histories* that were felt to be appropriate to this important marriage. The cassone made for the groom is decorated with suitably masculine subjects: Horatius Cocles Defending the Bridge (above) and Camillus Defeating the Gauls (on the front), and the side panels personify the male virtues of Justice and Fortitude. The bride's cassone was, by contrast, decorated with the characteristically feminine virtues of Prudence and Temperance. Large depictions of the Ordeal of Mucius Scaevola (above) and the Story of the Schoolmaster of Falerii (below) likewise contain relevant messages for a dutiful wife.

During the 15th century religion still dominated art and in overall appearance the cassoni, complete with their *spalliere*, resemble elongated altarpieces. Originally this evocation would have been even more striking because the base would have consisted of a panelled plinth painted with scenes, rather like a predella (altar-step). The carved feet in the form of a lion's paw are later additions, possibly from the 18th century.

Mystery surrounds most of the subsequent history of these pieces. They are known to have remained in the 17th century in the family for whom they were made, but after that the trail goes cold. Then, in the 1930s, they reappeared at a country auction in England, when they were sold by Sir Herbert Smith of Witley Park, Worcester, to an unknown buyer. In 1947 they were bought by Lord Lee of Fareham and later bequeathed to the Courtauld Institute in London, where they remain to this day.

Right **This interior view of the Nerli cassone shows the original decoration, which was stencilled in tempera. The highly stylized design was probably based on fabric patterns of the time.**

Overleaf **The Morelli (left) and Nerli (right) cassoni are the earliest known examples to survive complete with their back panels. Among the most prized pieces in the Italian Renaissance home, cassoni were also of practical use in holding household linen.**

85

86

Steel Chair
by Thomas Rucker

This unique seat is more than 400 years old and made entirely from chiselled steel. Every surface – back, front, and underneath – is encrusted with elaborate decoration. Myriad miniature pictorial scenes coat the ribs, three-dimensional sculptures adorn the base, and the back is formed with figural friezes illustrating stories from the Bible and classical mythology. One of the most unusual chairs ever made, it has a long history almost as complex and varied as the decoration with which it is covered.

Above **This detail of the elaborate pierced low-relief decoration on the back of the chair shows the dream of Nebuchadnezzar (left) and Daniel explaining it (right).**

88

The chair was made by Thomas Rucker (c.1532–1606), by whom it was signed and dated in 1574 and who must have regarded it as his masterpiece. An itinerant metalworker plying his trade in Augsburg, Dresden, and Vienna, Rucker was not in the habit of making such objects. Rather he is recorded as making sword hilts and scientific instruments, and he was particularly renowned for his odometers.

The identity and motives of the person responsible for commissioning the chair are uncertain, but it may have been made as a gift for an official of Augsburg's city council, perhaps for use on ceremonial occasions. This may explain the imposing throne-like form and the pine cone, the city's emblem, which surmounts the coat of arms at the back.

The chair was clearly meant to denote high office, and the subjects chosen to decorate it are intended to reinforce the status of its owner. Many of the scenes represent narratives of the four great monarchies of ancient civilization: Babylonian, Persian, Greek, and Roman, and the obvious message was that the occupant of such a seat perpetuated the spirit of such great dynasties. The meticulous style and the complex religious and mythological themes are typical of the mannerist era which bridges the gap between the Renaissance and baroque periods and mingles classical ideals with those of the Gothic tradition.

The subject-matter and meaning of many of the scenes may nowadays seem obscure, but the intricate detail remains as fresh and powerful as when the chair was first made. The

Left **The Emperor Rudolf II, portrayed by Johann or Hans von Aaachen. Rudolf preserved the steel chair in the treasury of his palace in Prague until it was seized by an invading Swedish army in 1648 and removed to Stockholm.**

Right **The subjects depicted on the chair include scenes from the Trojan Wars, executions, coronations, and genre scenes, and were probably adapted from contemporary prints. The sculpted figures standing on the back are Nebuchadnezzar (left) and Daniel (right).**

piece is supported on four elaborately scrolled legs, each ending in a curiously grotesque mask foot. Each leg is smothered in low-relief cartouches depicting narrative scenes divided by elaborate strapwork designs and heraldic emblems. Seated on platforms on two of the legs are sculptures of classical figures: Penelope and Ulysses; and Briseis and Achilles. Originally there would have been similar figures on the other two legs, but these have been lost (although one is now in the JW Higgins Armoury in Massachusetts). The four legs join with a central baluster that conceals a swivel joint connecting to the four ribs which provide the seat and arms. These too are copiously decorated with decorative cartouches and lead into the extremely elaborate back. Formed as a three-tiered temple, framed with classical pilasters, the pierced reliefs depict a triumphal procession, topped by the Dream of Nebuchadnezzar, with the Last Judgement and a portrait bust and Augsburg's arms above.

Augsburg was much acclaimed for its virtuoso furniture, a reputation of which it was proud, and examples of craftsmanship from the city were highly coveted by leading connoisseurs. In or around 1577 the steel chair was probably deemed important enough to be presented to the Emperor of the Holy Roman Empire, Rudolf II (1552–1612), by the civic authorities. Presumably delighted with his prestigious chair, Rudolf took it back to his palace in Prague, where for the next seven decades it remained the object of much admiration. An inventory of c.1610 described it as being "executed with the most highly skilled and exceptional workmanship".

In 1648 the Thirty Years War ended, but not before a triumphant Swedish army had swept into Prague, arriving at the Imperial Palace in July of that year. The palace had been emptied of many of its works of art, but among the trophies that remained the chair was captured as booty and dispatched back to Sweden. In Stockholm the trail once again becomes confused. The chair is thought to have been acquired by a Swedish general and was preserved in the capital's State Arsenal. By the mid-18th century it had again changed hands. This time it was sold at auction to an Anglo-Swedish antiquarian named Gustavus Brander. Born in London of Swedish parents, Brander had inherited a fortune from a relative and gave up his career in banking to become a keeper at the British Museum and pursue a life as a *cognoscente* collector.

Brander later settled in Christchurch, Hampshire, with his collection, including the chair. But the sea air harmed the metal and so Brander, concerned to preserve this unique piece, reluctantly sold it to another keen collector. According to family history, Brander was so attached to the chair that before his death in 1787 he made regular visits to its new home to inspect it. The extraordinary chair has been preserved, in unaltered condition, in the same private family collection ever since.

French Ebony Cabinet

Despite the temptation to see it as a highbrow piece of furniture, the subjects that decorate this 17th-century French cabinet were perhaps intended to be enjoyed more light-heartedly. Two racy novels of that period, L'Endymion *by Jean-Ogier Gombauld and* L'Ariane *by Jean Desmarets de Saint-Sorlin, provided the theme for the elaborate carving that fills the outer doors and base. The action-packed scenes must have made looking at the cabinet nearly as much fun as reading the books – and far less laborious.*

Above **The cabinet's inner doors open to reveal an architectural arrangement made from inlays of rosewood, ebony, and stained ivory. Most of the panels and drawers in the central section conceal hidden compartments.**

This massive cabinet, which is now in the Royal Collection at Windsor Castle, has many qualities that make it outstanding. It contains a multitude of layers, each packed with so many hidden surprises that it is almost impossible to list them all. In addition, it is a *tour de force* of carving and the complexity of the decoration is awe-inspiring – all the more so as ebony is one of the hardest and most awkward woods to carve with delicacy.

The precise history of the piece is unknown and over the years has been the subject of much speculation. At one time supposed to have belonged to Cardinal Wolsey, it was called the "Wolsey Cabinet". Then it was dubbed the "Rubens Cabinet", because its decoration was thought to have been based on drawings by the Flemish painter. It was also said to have been a gift from Louis XIV to Charles I of England.

Whatever its origins, the cabinet is the work of French craftsmen and dates from c.1640. Made from ebony veneered on to a softwood carcass, it has two massive hinged doors and stands on a matching ebonized fruitwood base with twelve elaborately carved legs. Unlock these outer doors and you come to another layer: two smaller central doors with drawers above and below and stacks of drawers on each side, with shallow slides at their base and across the centre. As you pull the slides you encounter the first surprise: they are not for writing – the central drawer is equipped for this – but inlaid for games such as chess and backgammon. The drawers above them are also inlaid with complex parquetry designs.

Above **The scenes which decorate the cabinet's second layer are inspired by engraved illustrations from the popular novel of the time, *L'Endymion*.**

90

The outer doors are carved with scenes taken from engraved illustrations from *L'Ariane*, a novel set in Rome. The sculpted figures standing inside the three niches probably represent the story's main characters – they pose rather like actors awaiting applause at the end of a play. The reverse of the doors is centred by octagonal panels depicting a loftier subject which may be a clue to the identity of the cabinet's original owner: the birth of Louis XIV to Anne of Austria. Inside the cabinet the scenes illustrate *L'Endymion*, a novel published in 1624 to wide acclaim. A similar cabinet in the Victoria & Albert Museum is also decorated with scenes from this book and it is thought that both pieces may once have belonged to Anne of Austria, who was fascinated by literature of the day.

Unlock the inner central cupboard and you find the cabinet's third layer. These doors are inlaid on their reverse with architectural parquetry and the central space is filled with an arrangement of painted panels, gilded corkscrew columns, and brass balustrades which is loosely based on the stage of a classical theatre. The panels, which are set at oblique angles to emphasize depth, and the tilted base reflect the 17th century's fascination with perspective and the creation of optical effects by manipulating space.

Nearly all the architectural elements of this inner layer can be removed or are themselves hidden compartments. There are four drawers behind the brass balustrade, and four more in the thin tortoiseshell moulding below it. The painted panels on each side can be pulled out to reveal further drawers, behind which are still more secret drawers.

The naturalistic painted panels seem out of keeping with the formal architectural style of the rest of the interior. In fact they are later replacements, perhaps put in to smarten up the cabinet in the 18th century, when it began to look tired. Painted in gouache on paper laid on to glass, they are the work of the 18th-century artist Charles-Louis Clérisseau, a favourite of English gentlemen on the Grand Tour. The original interior probably contained mirrors to emphasize the perspective and continue the architectural design of the inside of the doors, perhaps painted in oils or in marquetry similar to the doors.

Even in its present altered state the cabinet, which each year is seen and admired by thousands of visitors to the State Apartments at Windsor, is still as impressive as ever. Yet few of those who pause to admire the intricately carved scenes appreciate quite how risqué they must once have appeared.

Left **The cabinet may have been acquired for the Royal Collection in the 17th century, but the first definite record of the piece dates from 1825.**

91

Lignum Vitæ Cabinets

These cabinets are among the first and the most famous examples of the fashion for using lignum vitae as a veneer for furniture. Also known as guaiacum, lignum vitae ("wood of life") is a timber native to the West Indies that began to be imported into England during the 17th century after the Restoration. It is fine-grained and dark, has very pale sap wood and is so dense that it is one of the few timbers that sink in water. Veneers cut from branches sliced across the grain revealed extraordinary contrasting colours, and laid in striking mosaic-like patterns ("oyster veneering") created a decorative effect that was soon the height of fashion.

These cabinets were made c.1665 for the London apartments of the wife of Charles I of England, Queen Henrietta Maria, who was described by a contemporary as "a French lady of a haughty spiritt, and a greate witt and beauty". During the Civil War of 1642–6 Henrietta Maria escaped with her children to France. As the daughter of Henri IV of France, she rightly regarded her native country as a safe haven, and lived there in exile throughout England's Commonwealth. During this time she was accompanied by her secretary, Lord Henry Jermyn (later Earl of St Albans), with whom she enjoyed such intimacy that rumours abounded that she had secretly married him.

The cabinets probably date from the period when Henrietta Maria returned to England after the Restoration of the monarchy in 1660 and took up residence in Somerset House, beside the Thames. By now aged fifty, she was described by Samuel Pepys as a "very little plain old woman, and nothing more in her presence in any respect nor garb than any ordinary woman". Even so, she was given a huge allowance of £30,000 a year and was able to renovate her palatial residence and furnish it with characteristic French flair.

In style the cabinets show the influence of the Continent. The fine mouldings that border the drawers and occur in the central door are similar to northern European styles and

Right **One of the pair of striking lignum vitae, silver-mounted cabinets made for Queen Henrietta Maria and bequeathed by her to her confidant Lord Henry Jermyn. The oyster veneers capitalize on the wood's characteristically dramatic striations.**

Above **Charles I, Henrietta Maria, and Charles Prince of Wales by Hendrik Gerritszoon Pot; probably painted in 1632.**

strongly suggest the work of an immigrant craftsman. The materials used underline the fact that these pieces were prestigious items intended to display their owner's wealth and position. Lignum vitae was an extremely expensive wood, and less expensive pieces that followed this fashion were made from laburnum, which looked very similar but was indigenous to England and therefore far less costly. Another indication of the importance and preciousness of these cabinets is the abundance of silver mounts, which add greatly to the richness of their overall effect. In all there are ninety-eight, each one beautifully embossed with foliate decoration. Every drawer has a silver escutcheon; corners are encased in silver sheaths; scrolling silver pendants adorn the base; silver sleeves are wrapped at intervals around the legs; and the grand central silver plaque features Henrietta Maria's monogram: H.M.R. (Henrietta Maria Regina).

Perhaps the cabinets' most impressive feature is the way the craftsman has exploited the striking grain of the wood, using it in various ways to produce an eye-catching effect. On the front oysters have been cut in half to form a continuous pattern that looks like a series of linked "M"s. In the central panel the veneers are laid so that the colours radiate like a spoked wheel. On the sides is a chain-mail effect of linking loops made by whole slices of veneer. The frieze, plinth, and stretcher sides are veneered with wood cut parallel to the grain so that the effect is stripy. Made from the solid branch, the bobbin-turned legs are randomly patterned with the contrasting light and dark wood.

For all the elegance of her Somerset House apartments, Henrietta Maria did not stay there for long. She disliked life in England and hated the weather, and therefore in 1665 took up residence at Colombes, near Paris, where she remained until her death in 1669. On her departure from London for the last time it seems likely that the cabinets were given as a parting gift to her close friend Henry Jermyn. When he died in 1681 they passed to his nephew, Sir Thomas Jermyn of Rushbrooke Hall, Suffolk. They remained in the Rushbrooke family for the next two and a quarter centuries, until they were returned to the royal collection in 1910. A letter in Queen Mary's even handwriting, found at the back of one of the cabinets, fills in the last part of their story: "This pair of cabinets were sold by N. Rushbrooke Esq in 1910, and were bought by Lord Rothschild and his brother and presented to King George V and to Queen Mary and are now placed in the Vandyck Room at Windsor Castle." Appropriately, they now stand in the Queen's Ballroom at Windsor, a room made by Henrietta Maria's eldest son, Charles II, opposite a charming portrait by Sir Anthony Van Dyck of five of Henrietta Maria's children with their dogs.

93

Boulle Marquetry Cabinet on Stand

The luxuriant bouquets of flowers and minutely observed insects that adorn this stylish cabinet made c.1670 are so finely detailed, so fluid, and so naturalistic that you might imagine that they were painted rather than made from minute slivers of wood. This is wooden marquetry at its finest, and clearly the work of a highly accomplished craftsman. Indeed this magnificent cabinet is believed to have been made by the foremost ébéniste of the court of Louis XIV: André-Charles Boulle (1642–1732).

Above **The elaborate gilt bronze mount which surmounts the central panel comprises various military motifs ranged around a medallion by Jean Varin showing the profile of Louis XIV.**

Right **Like much of Boulle's early work the cabinet is in a heavily proportioned baroque style. The later work of the *ébéniste* is generally lighter and shows an increasing use of decorative arabesques.**

Boulle is best known for his metal and tortoiseshell marquetry, popularly known as "Boulle work", but during the earlier part of his career he specialized in the type of highly detailed wooden marquetry seen here. He had trained as a painter before turning his attention to furniture making and this partly explains the extraordinary pictorial qualities he managed to incorporate into his marquetry designs.

Although he himself was born in Paris, Boulle's family had originally emigrated to France from the Netherlands, where the art of exquisite marquetry flourished in the 17th century. Charles-André Boulle followed in his father's footsteps, becoming a master *ébéniste* before 1666. By the 1670s, when this cabinet was made, he had already attracted the attention of the king, and had been honoured by being granted a royal warrant and allowed to lodge and set up workshops in the prestigious Galerie du Louvre. Among the most important early royal commissions undertaken by Boulle were marquetry floors and panelling that he made for the Dauphin's apartments at Versailles, and for which he charged the considerable sum of nearly 100,000 livres.

Artists of the 17th century were fascinated by subjects drawn from natural history and by the still life. Flowers such as tulips and narcissi, which are featured here, were portrayed by leading artists of the day such as Jean-Baptiste Monnoyer, not only for their inherent beauty but also because they were great horticultural novelties and therefore extremely valuable. Boulle

was a keen collector of works of art and a huge proportion of his sizeable income from making furniture was spent on his passion for buying pictures, drawings, and prints. He accumulated a vast collection of studies of flowers and birds, some of which may have provided the inspiration for these designs.

Boulle is known to have made several cabinets of this type, all with slight variations. This one is among the numerous fine examples of French furniture in the Wallace Collection, and was purchased by Sir Richard Wallace; others are at the John Paul Getty Museum in California and in the collection of the Duke of Buccleuch at Drumlanrig Castle, Scotland. The cabinets fall into two groups: those with terminal supports – the sculpted figures have pedestal bases (of which this piece is an example) – and those with fully sculpted figures representing Hercules and his consort Omphale.

The cabinet is constructed on an oak carcass that is veneered in ebony, purple-wood, and tortoiseshell. Many other exotic woods, combined with brass, copper, and pewter, make up the complex designs. The supporting figures are carved from gessoed and painted pine. Sadly, the cabinet has suffered extensive alteration and somewhat unsympathetic renovation, probably when it was in the possession of the Parisian dealer A. Beurdeley before being bought by Sir Richard Wallace in 1872. How Beurdeley came by the cabinet is as yet unknown, although a piece this elaborate must have originated from an illustrious, if not royal, household.

The terminal figures supporting the base represent Ceres, the corn goddess, holding a sheaf of corn, and Bacchus, the god of wine, with his wreath of vine leaves. Both have been cut down and altered – the ears of corn have all but disappeared and Bacchus may originally have held a branch of vine under his crooked arm. The brown paint and gilding are also 19th-century modifications, since it is likely that the figures were originally painted in imitation stone or marble. Nevertheless, with their extravagantly curved draperies and naturalistically modelled bodies, they give the cabinet an engaging sculptural quality and a sense of movement that is continued in the curling fronds of foliage and flowers.

Boulle was also a keen collector of medals, often putting them in his furniture, and the medal at the top, which depicts the profile of the Sun King, Louis XIV, is by Jean Varin. The medal

Right **The naturalistic flowers that figure in the marquetry designs reflect the influence of the Flemish and Dutch craftsmen who brought this style of marquetry to France.**

95

can be unscrewed from its gilt metal mount and the reverse, which is dated 1664, shows a radiant sun, the emblem adopted by the monarch, shining down over the world, and is inscribed with his motto: *Nec pluribus impar* ("A match for many").

The interior of the cupboard is a slight disappointment and has been much changed. There are three angled mirrors, which probably date from the 19th century. One cannot help but think that originally there must have been a much more elaborate architectural arrangement. The floor, which is veneered with a shell design, and the door with its marquetry arabesques made from pewter and purple-wood, appear to be original. The large floral side panels, and those of the lower part of the cabinet, seem slightly less finely detailed than the central panel and may be the work of assistants.

Despite its numerous alterations and various problems, the cabinet is indisputably a feat of complex 17th-century crafts-manship; an awe-inspiring example of how, in the hands of an expert, flowers drawn from wood can rival the subtlety of those depicted in paint.

Far left **The terminal figures were probably inspired by Italian baroque sculpture. This figure, which represents Bacchus, the god of wine, has been reduced in size and repainted, probably in the late 19th century.**

Left **This piece, which is related to the Boulle cabinet, is in the collection of the Duke of Buccleuch at Drumlanrig Castle, Scotland, and dates from c.1670. The figural supports have also been repainted at a later stage with bronze paint; originally cream and gold paint would probably have been used.**

Right **Although the cabinet's early history is hitherto undiscovered, its imposing appearance is an indication that it was intended as a symbol of power and wealth, probably for a member of France's royal family.**

Chest-on-chest
by Lemon and McIntire

It is easy to see why this richly decorated mahogany chest-on-chest is called "the masterpiece of Salem". Its superb carving and striking architectural form place it among the finest examples of American furniture ever made. The piece was made in the town in 1796, probably by a local cabinet-maker named William Lemon, and was carved by another resident of Salem, Samuel McIntire (1757–1811).

Above **An exquisitely carved urn of fruit and flowers decorates the middle of the frieze. Most of the carving is believed to be by one of America's finest craftsmen, Samuel McIntire, and the crisply defined details attest to his outstanding expertise.**

Right **There are no obvious published designs for the chest-on-chest but the overall form of the piece relies heavily on traditional furniture patterns such as this one for a bureau bookcase, published in Chippendale's *The Gentleman and Cabinet-Maker's Director*.**

In the closing decades of the 18th century the port of Salem, north of Boston, was booming as a result of trade with the Far East. McIntire provided the newly prosperous with the region's answer to Robert Adam, being an architect, builder, carver, and designer in the neoclassical style that blossomed in America in the Federal period. McIntire was from a family of carpenters and carvers in Salem, and probably spent the early years of his training carving ship's figureheads and fittings for the busy local shipyards. A man blessed with a keen intellect, a dedicated scholar of architecture and a skilled musician, he enjoyed a career whose success owed much to his engaging and charismatic personality. After his death he was described as a "fine person, a majestic appearance, calm countenance, great self command and amiable temper".

McIntire was not only highly skilful; he was also extremely prolific. He designed and built some twenty mansions in and around Salem, including one for Elizabeth Derby, for whom he also made this chest-on-chest. Elizabeth was the daughter of Elias Hasket Derby, one of Boston's wealthiest merchants and a keen patron of local cabinet-makers (*see page 103*).

Tradition has it that the chest-on-chest was a wedding gift to Elizabeth from her father on her marriage to Captain Nathaniel West. Traditionally, the piece has been associated with one listed on a bill dated 22 October 1796, from Samuel McIntire and William Lemon to Elizabeth Derby West. However, the discrepancy between the amount of carving mentioned on the bill and that on this exceptionally elaborately decorated chest has recently caused experts to doubt whether the pieces are in fact one and the same. Nonetheless, the quality and style

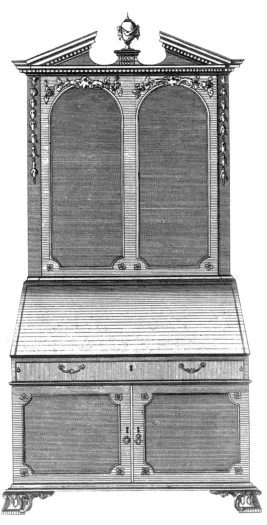

of the carving are still widely considered to be clear indications of the superlative craftmanship of Samuel McIntire.

The chest is made from "crotch" mahogany, a term which means the veneers were cut from the join between the trunk and a main branch of the tree, giving the striking swirling figured wood. Veneering became more commonplace at this time because methods of cutting the thin slices of wood improved dramatically. The veneers here are laid on to a carcass of pine – standard secondary wood for east coast furniture.

In size and shape the chest-on-chest is based on the sturdy designs of the Chippendale period that appeared in Thomas Chippendale's influential pattern book *The Gentleman and Cabinet Maker's Director* and were widely available to American cabinet-makers of the time. The carving is in the neo-classical style that McIntire loved, and marks a departure from the florid, curving forms of rococo style that had dominated the appearance of the finest furniture made earlier in the century. A wide band dividing the upper and lower parts is decorated with alternating fluting and rosettes, both of which are classical motifs. Seen from the front, the upper part of the piece reads like a temple façade. The drawers are framed on each side by fluted columns and crowned by a central broken pediment.

Many of the elaborately carved decorations seen here were McIntire favourites also used to decorate the houses on which he worked. The carving of the frieze is especially skilful. In the centre there is an urn overflowing with fruit, while on each side are cherubs holding baskets on their heads. These figures are usually interpreted as symbols of hope and plenty in the new republic, but if the wedding-gift story is true perhaps they also represent fertility and prosperity within the marriage.

Above the frieze is the final crowning glory. The figure of Nike, Greek goddess of Victory, towers over the centre of the broken pediment. Recent research suggests that she may be the work of another Boston family of wood carvers, the Skillins. Once gleaming, Nike's gilding has faded only slightly, and she remains the perfect crowning ornament for such an outstanding example of wood carving.

Left **The chest-on-chest's imposing appearance relies on the combination of sturdy outline, delicate carving, and richly figured wood. Although growing doubt surrounds the documentation with which it has long been associated, the piece is still rightly seen as one of the masterpieces of American craftsmanship.**

99

The Venus and Diana Commodes

"A drawing room worthy of Eve before the Fall" was how Horace Walpole, after his visit to Osterley Park in 1773, described his impression of the interior, where these elegant commodes took centre stage. Decorated with panels showing Venus and Diana, they are classical furniture at its most elaborate and sumptuous. Although the identity of the craftsman responsible for the commodes remains questionable, the delicacy of the marquetry inlays and the elaborately chased metal mounts are signs of an outstanding talent.

Above **The rather severe semi-elliptical shape of the commodes is softened by the elaborate gilt-metal mounts and complex marquetry with which they are decorated, and reflects the influence of French neoclassical furniture.**

When Walpole visited Osterley Park, west of London, it was the home of Robert Child, a member of the wealthy banking family. Throughout the 18th century, under various members of the family, the house had been outwardly transformed from Tudor mansion to classical-style villa and the interiors were also updated to conform to the latest and most expensive taste. Many of the interiors and items of furniture, including these commodes, were designed by the celebrated architect Robert Adam, Britain's leading exponent of the neoclassical style.

The rebuilt house has been described as a pantheon of the arts and sciences, and Robert Adam's elegantly designed interiors are full of allusions to classical art, architecture, and literature, taking for granted a wide knowledge of such subject-matter. Such refinement was intended to establish the Child family, whose fortune from banking had only recently been amassed, as a family of gentility and discernment.

The drawing-room brims with classical references. The ceiling's plasterwork is derived from the Temple of the Sun at Palmyra and the same pattern is mirrored in the carpet. The commodes do not pretend to have any practical purpose – there are no cupboards in them, nothing opens; they are simply meant to be seen as a striking component in a beautiful decorative scheme. Forming part of a typical 18th-century room arrangement, they stand against the wall between windows with elegant pier glasses above. With their softly muted colours, decorations borrowed from classical antiquity, and a

Above **The central marqetry roundel depicts Venus and Cupid. This panel is framed by strips of a green veneer known as harewood, which is made by staining sycamore or maple with iron oxide.**

sophisticated elliptical shape, they glow with refinement. However, when they were first made their effect was not nearly so subtle. Adam loved surprisingly rich colour schemes and the notes on preparatory drawings for the commodes suggest that originally he intended them to be painted with a dark-green background. Instead some of the wood (the striations within the hexagonal frame surrounding the central medallions) was harewood stained bright green so that they matched the colour of the walls. Lady Beauchamp Proctor wrote in 1772 of her impressions: "a beautiful room, hung with pea-green damask, furniture the same, the ceiling is extremely elegant, painted and gilt, and the carpet, which is from Mr Moores manufactory answers to the ceiling".

The decoration of these pieces is repeated around the rest of the room. Their friezes have central plaques with a classical profile medallion, griffons, and acanthus scrolls. The same frieze occurs above the door, and a similar one in the chimney-piece, while the arched metal border at the base echoes the frieze around the ceiling. The identity of the maker remains the subject of speculation. Both John Linnell (*see* pages 56–9) and Ince and Mayhew have been suggested, while the Swedish cabinet-maker Christopher Fuhrlohg, a contemporary of Georg Haupt (*see* pages 124–5), may have had a hand in the execution of the marquetry medallions.

These panels take love as their theme: one shows Venus, goddess of sensual love, with the attendant Cupid; the other features Diana the huntress, the personification of chastity. Both subjects were adapted from engravings after popular paintings by Angelica Kauffmann, while the classical figures in the flanking oval medallions were inspired by frescos recently discovered at Herculaneum.

Love was to prove a thorny subject for the Child family. At the age of eighteen Robert Child's only daughter, Sarah Anne, was smitten by the dangerous charms of the Earl of Westmorland. Realizing that her parents were against the match, "Rapid Westmorland" eloped with his bride-to-be in the small hours of the morning and made a dash for Gretna Green. Sarah's father, on discovering that the couple were missing, gave chase and his horsemen caught up with them. "Rapid" fired at Child's party, killing a horse, and managed to escape. He married Sarah the next day in an alehouse. The shock of the affair can have done nothing to improve Child's delicate health. He died a few months later, but not before changing his will to punish his wayward daughter.

Right **The hollow commodes are still positioned as they were in Robert Adam's day, with pier glasses above. The** **pieces were intended purely for decoration, and bring together classical motifs used elsewhere in the room.**

Commode by John and Thomas Seymour

With a top resembling a setting sun and dramatic stripes of dark and light wood on the sides, this commode is among the most elegant pieces of furniture made in Boston in the late 18th or early 19th centuries. John Seymour, its designer, has used many imaginative decorative details to transform the simple semicircular form into an exceptional piece. Among these are exquisitely painted shells in a medallion, handsome lion's-head handles, unusually shaped legs with lion's-paw feet, and stunningly figured veneers.

Right **John Seymour and his son Thomas are well known for the way in which they used contrasting veneers to create a striking effect. Time and exposure to sunlight have made the variations in the woods' colours seem subtle, but originally they would have been far more eye-catching.**

Above **In the early part of the 19th century, Boston, seen here c.1840, experienced a sustained growth in prosperity. This created a ready demand for fashionable furniture and the city soon became one of America's major centres of furniture making.**

102

The design of the piece is equally ingenious: there are four drawers in the centre and the sides look as if they follow suit, but in fact they are false drawer fronts on hinged doors that hide small cupboards on each side. The commode dates from 1809, from a period known in American furniture history as "Federal", when the country's new political independence was marked by increased prosperity, particularly in thriving trading centres such as Boston.

The Federal period of furniture was characterized by the development of Americanized versions of the classical designs of influential English cabinet-makers such as Sheraton and Hepplewhite. In place of the undulations, flowery carving, and japanned decoration that had earlier been so fashionable, shapes became simpler, lighter, and more elegant, and regional differences became more pronounced. Cabinet-makers in Boston increasingly used imported woods for visual interest.

Had he seen the Boston commode, Sheraton would have probably recognized a marked similarity to designs that he had published in his pattern books. He would certainly have approved of the classic demi-lune shape; the use of satinwood, particularly if it was adorned, as here, with painted decoration; and he often used shells for marquetry inlay. Conversely, the reeded columns, the choice of secondary woods such as pine, maple, and chestnut, and the oddly shaped bulbous legs and lion's-paw feet would have been less familiar to him, and give the piece a pronounced American identity.

Above **The artist responsible for creating the detailed and striking painting of seashells that decorates the top of the commode is mentioned on the original bill of sale for the piece. His name is given as John Ritto Pennimen, a Boston-based painter.**

By the time this commode was made, Boston, thanks to booming trade and prosperous merchants with money to spend on building and furnishing their houses, had become a major furniture-making centre. The area had several leading cabinet-makers, of whom one of the finest was John Seymour. Born in England, Seymour emigrated to Maine with his son Thomas in 1785 and, within a few years of settling in Boston, enjoyed a reputation for producing top-quality furniture. Thomas joined the business from the turn of the century, although it seems

likely that Seymour senior continued to be the driving force in terms of design. The Seymours specialized in furniture of great sophistication and delicacy. Fashionable tambour (cylindrical) shutters were a favourite, as was the demi-lune pattern, used to dramatic effect on the top of this piece.

The story of the Seymour commode can be followed thanks to the surviving bill of sale, which records that it was sold by Thomas to Elizabeth Derby. Elizabeth was the daughter of Elias Hasket Derby, a wealthy Boston merchant (*see* page 98).

The woods used to decorate the commode reflect the fashion for expensive imports. The exterior is veneered in a combination of mahogany, satinwood, bird's-eye maple, and rosewood. Inside, on the invisible areas, indigenous secondary timbers were used: white pine, curly maple, and chestnut. Striking today, the effect must have seemed even more so a century or so ago, when such brilliant and exotic woods, unsubdued by sunlight, must have brought a generous helping of colour, as well as cachet, to Elizabeth Derby's elegantly furnished home.

Pietre Dure Commode by Martin Carlin

Extremely colourful in both its history and its appearance, this commode is encrusted with nineteen pietre dure plaques, each of which is decorated with jewel-like fruits and flowers carved from a variety of brilliantly coloured stones. It is no coincidence that the panels resemble so closely those that decorate the Badminton Cabinet (see pages 32–5), because the commode is a marriage of the work of craftsmen of two centuries. The ravishing fruit-garnished panels were made towards the close of the 17th century, while the commode that provides their framework is in the most fashionable style of nearly a hundred years later.

Above **Seven low-relief plaques – here a detail of two of them is shown – decorate the front of the commode. Each plaque is encrusted with a variety of carved stone fruits and foliage.**

Made c.1775, this lavish piece is one of the masterpieces of Martin Carlin (c.1730–85). Among the leading French *ébénistes* of the late 18th century, Carlin was particularly accomplished at incorporating all sorts of materials into his furniture designs. Porcelain plaques made by Sèvres and precious panels of imported oriental lacquer were often assimilated into his sophisticated designs (*see* pages 30–1). The *pietre dure* plaques he uses here originate from the Gobelins workshops in Paris, where in the late 17th century Gian-Ambrogio Giachetti, an Italian craftsman from Florence (the leading European centre for the production of *pietre dure*), had helped French craftsmen to set up a *pietre dure* manufactory. Giachetti's signature is scratched on the back of two of the plaques.

The plaques illustrated here were not originally intended to decorate a piece of furniture of this form, for the simple reason that commodes had not yet become fashionable as pieces of furniture in the 1680s, when they were made. They were almost certainly cannibalized from a cabinet. However, a century later, furnishing fashion had moved on, and apart from one or two noteworthy exceptions (*see* pages 42–5), cabinets were passé, while in an elegantly appointed salon a commode was generally considered to be much more stylish. By contrast, *pietre dure* panels were still regarded as great rarities and thus highly

Académie Impériale de Musique.

Mlle Laguerre.

Left **Marie-Josephine Laguerre, here depicted in an engraving, was a famous opera star whose penchant for romance enabled her to build up an enviable collection of fine furniture, including Carlin's *pietre dure* commode.**

Right **Carlin applied the *pietre dure* plaques to an oak carcass veneered with mahogany. The break-fronted design and gilt bronze swags decorating the frieze are very characteristic of his luxurious furniture.**

prized. Therefore it is not at all surprising to find an *ébéniste* of Carlin's repute reusing old materials in an up-to-date design.

Seven three-dimensional panels have been inset into the cabinet's front, which is composed of a central cupboard with what appear to be three drawers on each side. These "drawers" are, in fact, false and the narrow panels are also set into cupboard doors. Each side of the commode is adorned with six flat *pietre dure* panels filled with flowers and fruit, and these stone pictures, rainbow-like in appearance and combined with the most sumptuous gilding imaginable, are set against a striking ebony-veneered backdrop.

Like many other *ébénistes* of the period, Carlin rarely made furniture for private customers but instead was chiefly employed supplying furniture to leading *marchand-merciers* (furniture dealers), who in turn sold it on to their fashionable clientele. In this case he probably made the piece for the dealer Dominique Daguerre. It then found its way into the luxurious home of one of the most rapacious and fast-living courtesans of the day, Marie-Josephine Laguerre, perhaps as a gift from one of her besotted admirers. A lover of wine, romance, and music, Marie-Josephine was a star at the Paris Opéra and attracted the attentions of numerous well-to-do gentlemen whom she

encouraged to shower her with lavish tokens of affection such as this commode. When she died at the age of twenty-eight, after an action-packed life, she left in her wake two mansions, top-quality furniture, and an amazing array of jewels.

At a posthumous sale of Marie-Josephine's property the commode was purchased by a wealthy collector, Baron de Dezonval. It was later acquired for George IV of England by his assistant Benois (who had acquired several other outstanding pieces of French furniture for him) in the early years of the 19th century. It now stands, as spectacular as ever, in the Green Drawing Room of Buckingham Palace.

Micro-mosaic Table by Achilles Taddei

At first sight the vividly coloured flowers that garland this table and enclose the goldfinches fluttering in its centre appear to have been brilliantly and naturalistically rendered in paint. However, if you examine the piece closely you can see that each petal and each bird is in fact depicted by minute slivers of glass set into a black marble ground. This astonishing technique, known as micro-mosaics, was from the 18th century a specialty of craftsmen working in Rome, where the top of this table was made c.1830.

Above **Intended to simulate the appearance of painting, micro-mosaics are built up from thousands of minute slivers of coloured glass, inlaid on a stone background and then polished to give their spectacular effect.**

The art of micro-mosaics was both inspired and paralleled by the 18th-century fascination with the world of antiquity, and in particular the artefacts of ancient Rome. It developed hand in hand with the increasingly popular practice of excavating antique Roman mosaics, which fuelled a renewal of interest in the long-forgotten technique. Fragments of ancient Roman micro-mosaics were highly sought after by wealthy Englishmen who were making the Grand Tour, but demand for the precious relics far exceeded supply, with the result that before long a ready market for imitations had developed.

While Florence dominated the production of inlays made from *pietre dure* – which literally means "hard stone" (*see* pages 104–5) – the manufacture of micro-mosaics was centred in Rome. This technique was developed in the Vatican workshops, where, during the early 18th century, dilapidated altarpieces in St Peter's were replaced by giant mosaic pictures. Interest in the technique spread as mosaics began to be used to decorate furniture, and table tops and other objects were produced by the Vatican workshops, initially as papal and diplomatic gifts.

By the 19th century the Roman micro-mosaic industry was firmly established and ateliers elsewhere began producing similar pieces as these impressive pictorial scenes became increasingly coveted. Micro-mosaics were supplied to many royal courts. Napoleon in particular was a great admirer and during his Italian campaign ordered pieces for the Quirinale Palace in Rome. These included a table referred to as

Left **The heavy, leaf-encrusted, gilt-bronze pedestal that forms the base of the table was probably made in England c.1830, when the top was brought back as a souvenir of Rome.**

Right **A wreath of flowers encircles a pair of chaffinches holding an intertwined ribbon. The romantic nature of this subject-matter suggests that the table was designed as an allegory of love or marriage.**

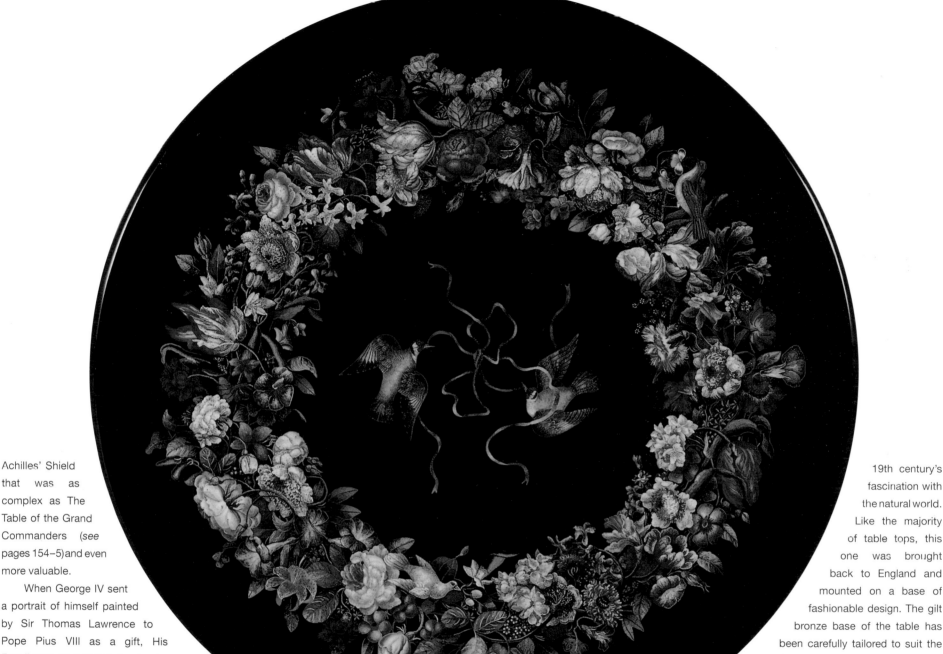

Achilles' Shield that was as complex as The Table of the Grand Commanders (*see* pages 154–5) and even more valuable.

When George IV sent a portrait of himself painted by Sir Thomas Lawrence to Pope Pius VIII as a gift, His Excellency responded by having a copy of the portrait executed in micro-mosaic by Domenico Moglia as an offering to the English king. The portrait, which contains some half a million glass fragments, now hangs in the Royal Pavilion in Brighton. Circular table tops were among the most popular souvenirs of the Grand Tour, and such was the interest in micro-mosaics that two tables were exhibited at the Great Exhibition in London in 1851. Many fine examples are on display in the Gilbert Collection, Los Angeles County Museum.

Whereas antique mosaics were usually made from marble and stone, by the early 19th century craftsmen in Rome had perfected the technique of creating complex designs using slices of glass so minute that they had to handle them with tweezers. The extremely subtle effect was intended to simulate painting. Craftsmen had at their disposal a range of about 20,000 extremely fine gradations in tone, which allowed them to depict light and shade very effectively.

An enormous variety of designs was used to decorate micro-mosaic tables. Classical subjects were drawn from art and literature while picturesque landscapes or architectural subjects provided impressive mementoes of famous Italian landmarks, or, as in this case, floral compositions reflect the 19th century's fascination with the natural world. Like the majority of table tops, this one was brought back to England and mounted on a base of fashionable design. The gilt bronze base of the table has been carefully tailored to suit the top's naturalistic theme, with foliate plumes and a scrolled leaf base.

Little is known of Achilles Taddei, the highly skilled artist whose signature is inscribed on the table top, but his virtuoso flower-filled design is similar to that of tables made by other leading micro-mosaicists such as Camillo Poggioli and Gioacchino Barberi. Roses, tulips, convolvuli, poppies, pinks, forget-me-nots, and narcissi mingle together in glorious and almost tactile abundance, their brilliant colours emphasized by the polished black marble into which they are inlaid. The pair of gold finches in the centre holding a pink ribbon suggest that the subject may be intended as an allegory of love. It is tempting to imagine that the top was brought back from Italy by a romantically inclined traveller as an earnest of affection for his loved one.

107

Sofa by John Henry Belter

Above **A typical mid-19th-century parlour at Bayou Bend, Houston, Texas, is furnished with Belter pieces and shows the rather cluttered, heavily patterned style that prevailed in many homes at that time.**

Right **Belter's original patent, which was registered in New York in 1858, explains diagrammatically his ingenious method of laminating and moulding wood.**

Around the middle of the 19th century no fashionable New York home was thought complete without a piece of furniture by John Henry Belter. This extravagant sofa is a great rarity, but during that period Belter made a substantial amount of similar, although less elaborate, seating, and such was the demand for his furniture that he came to be known as "America's most fashionable cabinet-maker".

Right **Much of the intricate wood carving on pieces such as this sofa was carried out by German craftsmen, who were highly accomplished in the art.**

Like most of Belter's furniture, this piece is both generous and curvaceous, and has not a single straight line. Its most striking feature is undoubtedly the carving which covers almost every visible part of the frame, for Belter delighted in carved ornament of great complexity. The back is encrusted with bouquets of richly carved flowers, lacy scrolls, trailing naturalistic foliage, acorns, oak leaves, and vines laden with bunches of grapes. These are carved in such profusion that, unlike almost any other sofa style, the frame almost overpowers the upholstery.

How did Belter manage to bend wood into such bizarre shapes, and then pierce it so extensively, without sacrificing its strength? He developed and patented an ingenious method of producing moulded laminated wood – a forerunner of what we know today as plywood – which anticipated the bentwood furniture of 20th-century avant-garde designers. He took veneers of wood 1/16in (1.5mm) thick and sandwiched them together so that the grain of each veneer ran at right angles to that of those adjacent to it. Between six and sixteen layers were used to make a material strong enough to withstand the moulding process and thick enough for carving. The laminate was then steamed to soften it, moulded into curved shapes, and carved.

The laminated wood had three important advantages: it used expensive veneers (mainly rosewood) more economically; the furniture was relatively light for its size; and it was strong. (If solid wood is carved and pierced in this way it becomes extremely fragile.)

Belter's flamboyant decoration was certainly not for the faint-hearted, but at the time it was an effective antidote to the sober classical styles of previous decades. His designs ignore

J. H. BELTER.
MANUFACTURING FURNITURE.

No. 19,405.   Patented Feb. 23, 1858.

the slender, rectilinear elegance and the antique motifs that had been employed by furniture makers of the Empire and Federal periods. For inspiration he turned instead to the exuberant, swirling French rococo furniture styles of the mid-18th century, reinterpreting them in his uniquely lavish way.

Belter was born in Germany and had emigrated to America in 1833. By the middle of the century he was providing the homes of the *nouveaux riches* of New Orleans, New York, and Baltimore with deliciously unrestrained decoration and plush upholstery which especially appealed to the taste of families of French origin. At this time the population was mushrooming, and in consequence there was an unprecedented demand for

furniture. Belter had a large workshop where he employed about forty apprentices and where furniture-making, although still a hand-crafted process, was streamlined and standardized in order to increase production. His business continued to thrive until his death in 1863, when it was taken over by a member of his family and renamed Springmeier Bros.

An unusual feature of this and other Belter sofas is the fact that the back is also faced with finished figured wood. It is unusual to find this detail on earlier sofas, which were designed to stand against a wall. As the practice of permanently placing furniture in the centre of a room caught hold in the 19th century, furniture adapted to suit the new trend.

Sofas in the mid-19th century were usually produced as part of a parlour suite which typically included several matching armchairs as well as another sofa and a centre table. The newly affluent householders of Belter's day wanted their interiors to look both lusciously coloured and comfortable. Upholstered furniture contributed greatly to the sumptuous appearance of the parlour and one great advance in its construction in the early decades of the century was the invention of sprung upholstery. On this sofa the back is also deeply padded and buttoned to add to this effect. Although the upholstery and damson damask covering are replacements, they were selected to reflect the preference of Belter and his contemporaries for rich colours.

Chairs by John Makepeace

Above **Each part of the Millennium Chair's complex curving form and web-like back is made from eleven layers of laminated holly.**

The driving force behind the revival of interest in hand-crafted furniture, John Makepeace occupies a pivotal place in the recent development of British furniture design. His view that craftsmanship can still surpass machine production has manifested itself through his furniture and through the School for Craftsmen in Wood, at Parnham House. This college, which he started, has given its students the training to enable them to pursue successful careers as furniture designers. Chairs, Makepeace believes, are one of the most fundamental and personal types of furniture as their shape must reflect the human form to support it satisfactorily.

Below **The whimsical Knot Chair's arms and legs are English oak, while its carved seat and back are burr elm.**

Right **The painted Vine Chair combines traditional carving techniques with an original approach to design.**

Far right **Made in 1978, the Mitre Chair reinterprets a Gothic shape in 20th-century techniques and materials.**

Like many furniture designer-makers, Makepeace trained as a craftsman in wood, although in recent years his designs have been realized by a team of craftsmen who operate from a workshop at Parnham House, Dorset, the site of the renowned school of woodworking. The Mitre Chair, dating from 1978, was one of Makepeace's most notable early successes. Made from more than 2000 pieces of ebony, it has a sinuously elegant shape that reflects the designer's absorption of Gothic and art nouveau forms. At the same time the complex layered construction and the nickel silver with which the woven seat and back are constructed are inescapably the legacy of 20th-century technological advancement.

Natural forms and organic shapes have become increasingly dominant features of Makepeace's furniture. At first sight the Millennium Chair appears not unlike the earlier Mitre Chair in the purity of its shape, but its design pays homage to the human form itself rather than reflecting architectural precedents. The delicate striations in the pale layered holly from which the chair is made suggest a skeletal form, much like Gaudí's strange constructions for the Casa Calvet (*see* pages 172–3). Every element in the design is tailored to reflect and support the human spine: the chair has been described as "a three-dimensional graph of the curvature of the human back".

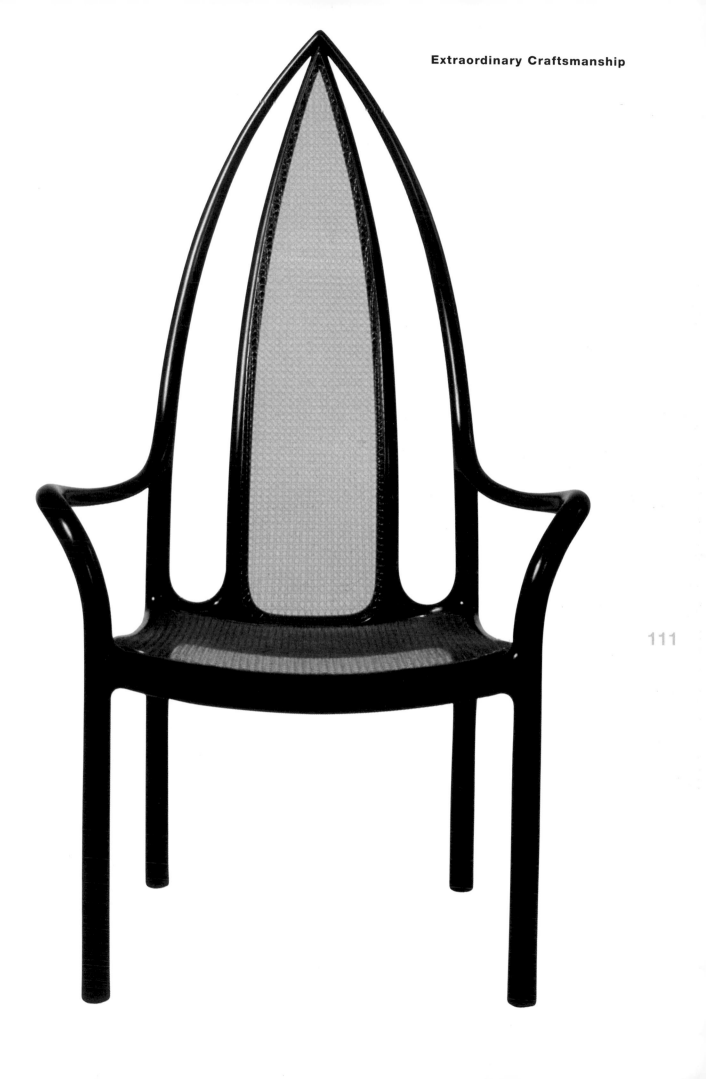

Three-dimensional illusionism is a more obvious feature of the Knot Chair, whimsically carved from English oak and burr elm to look as if seat and back are made from a knotted cushion. Like Wendell Castle, his American contemporary and friend (*see* pages 178–9), Makepeace combines sculptural forms and techniques with furniture, and in doing so he challenges conventional boundaries as well as our perception of softness and hardness, comfort and discomfort. The chair was designed for an American collector who thought this version too faded in colour and wanted a richer tone. It is now in a private collection in Hong Kong.

One of the most dramatic and challenging of Makepeace's recent designs is the Vine Chair. Carved from lime wood and painted by Adrian Everett, this reflects Makepeace's growing environmental concerns. Wood, the stock-in-trade of the furniture maker, is in limited supply, so Makepeace stopped making pieces from imported tropical hardwoods several years ago and now uses only indigenous varieties. Nevertheless he realizes that stocks of many native British woods, and in particular burr varieties, are also limited. For this reason he now encourages his craftsmen to consider ways to enhance the appearance of furniture made from varieties of timber that are readily available and renewable but less naturally spectacular.

Painting furniture is one of the most obvious ways to make wood look more visually interesting. Carved in the form of an illusionistic tree, with leaf-encrusted back and seat and tree-trunk legs and frame, this chair is, like all these examples, far more than just something to sit on. Its powerful design demands to be seen also as a work of art; as a statement of Makepeace's concern for the survival of the forest; and as a declaration of the progress of hand-crafted furniture.

111

Walnut Pedestal Sideboard

The starting point for the commission we received to design and make an impressive sideboard for a dining-room was the purchase of an Alfred Dunhill humidor. After taking his cigar box home the gentleman decided that he needed something on which to stand it. He commissioned a small trolley that would allow the humidor to be pushed around the dining-table. However, after deciding that the design was not sufficiently imposing, he rethought the commission and asked us to design a sideboard instead.

Right **Walnut is the primary wood used for the sideboard, but the columns are of solid satinwood and a boxwood section divides the arch from the lower section.**

Bottom right **Our second drawing used Inigo Jones as the inspiration for a classical design with a modern feel.**

Above **The marquetry armorials which fill the central niche of each pedestal match those which decorate the antique dining chairs.**

Right **The fronts of the pedestal support are hinged and can be opened to reveal storage cupboards. In addition, a drawer is concealed in the plinth below.**

The sideboard was to stand in a large, square dining-room in a country house which had recently been built in traditional English style. It was to replace an existing side table whose stunning green marble top was to be incorporated in the new piece of furniture. The dimensions of the sideboard were therefore governed by the size of the marble top. The height was also an important consideration, since the new piece was to stand beneath a large oil painting.

We did not want the lid of the cigar box which was to sit on the sideboard to strike the canvas above it when it was raised. Nevertheless we decided that it was necessary to raise the height of the sideboard slightly to match the level of the dado and to create a slight break in the powerful horizontal line of the painting's frame. The other notable pieces of furniture in the room which played a role in the finished design were a beautiful set of walnut dining chairs whose back splats were inlaid with the family coat of arms.

The design of the cigar box had been inspired by the buildings of Inigo Jones, who, in the 17th century, was one of the first architects to introduce the principles of classical architecture to England. We decided to continue the Inigo Jones theme in the style of the sideboard. Our first attempt was a frank pastiche of theatrical baroque-style furniture, complete with lavishly carved festoons, swags, and a grand central coat of arms. But we felt that the drawing lacked excitement, and in our second, successful design we drew directly from Jones's architecture, using

some of his favourite motifs and reinterpreting them in a fresh way in the form of furniture.

We gave the piece a sculptural, three-dimensional look by creating a solid walnut frieze carved with alternating metopes and triglyphs and by using three-dimensional flanking columns in satinwood to punctuate the façades of the pedestal bases. The niches, with their look of rusticated quoining, were made by dividing the walnut with inlaid strips of box. In the centre of each niche, on a satinwood ground, the family coat of arms was copied with great care from the walnut dining chairs. The pedestals also serve a practical purpose, since their fronts are hinged and conceal cupboards. The result is a powerful design which bridges the gap between the traditional and the modern. We hope that even Inigo Jones might have approved.

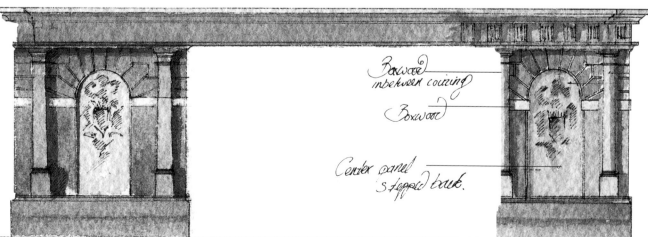

Extraordinary Inventiveness
mechanical and multipurpose furniture

The desire to create pieces that were both novel and versatile has inspired some of the most intriguing furniture ever made. Mechanical desks with secret compartments were among the most complex mechanical pieces made in the 18th century, and, as the taste grew for furniture both luxurious and intriguing, other ingenious pieces came into being. While practicality played a major role in some designs, in others the aim was to display the maker's virtuosity and the owner's discerning taste.

Left **This elaborate French mechanical table c.1760–5 is veneered with tulipwood and inlaid with various exotic timbers. The piece contains a writing flap that opens to allow the back section to rise mechanically, revealing a nest of drawers, compartments, and a detachable reading stand.**

Sleeping Chair

For the dignitary visiting a grand house in the 17th century the interminable strain of receiving guests and granting audiences would have been considerably diminished by this ingenious piece of furniture. Chair and daybed in one, it allowed its user to sit in regal upright pose when entertaining guests, and then, when stupor took over, to lower the back-rest and doze or read in comfort. The chair is one of a pair made c.1670 for Ham House, south-west of London, one of the grandest of English 17th-century houses and the home of one of the most extravagant ladies of the day, Elizabeth, Duchess of Lauderdale.

Below **The Duchess of Lauderdale, depicted here with the Duke by Peter Lely, had a huge appetite for luxurious furniture, patronizing both English and continental makers. Within ten years of marrying she had almost fully refurnished Ham House.**

Above **Ham House, seen here from the north front, was built in 1610 by an unknown architect and extensively enlarged by the Duke and Duchess of Lauderdale.**

Chairs have long denoted social status, and the throne-like appearance of this one, achieved in part by the sumptuous fabric with which it is covered, is an unmistakable signal of its user's importance. This is a chair reserved for none but the most noble of visitors. It was ordered by the Duchess as a centre-piece for the Queen's Closet, an intimate but lavishly decorated room among a suite of staterooms specially decorated in the 1660s for Queen Catherine of Braganza, the wife of Charles II of England. The sleeping chair is typical of the extravagant furnishings that were acquired by the Duchess of Lauderdale. The second marriage of this flame-haired beauty, to one of the country's most powerful men, John, 2nd Duke of Lauderdale, Charles II's Secretary of State for Scotland, spurred her desire to double the size of Ham House in order to make it into an exceptionally grand country residence .

The comfortably padded chair is still covered with its original raspberry-coloured brocade, which was splendidly embroidered with gold thread to match the brocade lining the walls. The chair's seat, arms, and lower back were elaborately trimmed with a glittering metallic fringe fixed in place by gilt nails. The straight, boxy appearance of the upper part of the piece is in complete contrast to the undulating elements from which the lower frame is made. The feet are carved as sea

horses on whose muscular backs rest the spiralling legs. These in turn are joined and strengthened by a front stretcher in the form of an elaborate scroll with a pair of cherubs clutching a bunch of grapes in the centre.

The chair was operated by means of two gilded metal quadrants attached to the underside of the arms and to the back of the seat, which allowed the user to tilt the back and fix it in position with a small metal pin. However, despite the lavish decoration and innovative design, the piece was not a complete success. If the occupant stood up suddenly when the back of the chair was fully tilted, the base was not heavy enough to keep it stable. As a result, the whole thing would topple over backwards – a design fault that surely occasioned some very undignified scenes. Although two chairs were ordered for the Queen's Closet they did not fit comfortably in the tiny room side by side, and the small alcove in which the chair stood was not wide enough to allow the back to recline and still face forwards.

Even so, the effect of the chair's rich colours, exuberant carving, and rich gilding must have created a fine spectacle. Indeed the entire room, even down to the parquetry design on the floor, is organized to draw the eye to the focal point – the occupant of the chair. Visitors who saw the newly executed decorations at Ham could not have failed to be overawed. The diarist John Evelyn likened it to a royal palace "furnished like a Great Prince's", while the architect Roger North said of the state apartments: "there are all the rooms of parade, exquisitely plact … so that the visto is compleat from end to end."

Sadly, the Duchess of Lauderdale's social status, along with her reputation as a doyenne of good taste, was short-lived. Thanks to the enormous sums she had squandered on Ham and her other residences, she found herself in severe financial difficulty when her husband died in 1682, only a decade after their marriage. Forced to pawn or sell many of her most valued possessions in order to make ends meet, she retired from court to live in seclusion at Ham. Before she died, in 1694, she described her last days in a poignant letter to her daughter: "It is now more than 8 years since I have been so constantly fixed in this place that I am even a stranger to all others … I have never yet been farther than this lowe story … all my movable estate is sould (even to the disfurnishing of this my dwelling house) … and now what can I or what must I further do? But condemn my own mistaken measurs which have proved so fatal."

Right **The chair has been miraculously well preserved with its original upholstery and trimmings. Made for the Queen's Closet, one of the most luxurious of the state apartments at Ham, it has fine decoration that served to complement the wall hangings of "crimson and gould stuff bordered wth. green and gould and silver stuff".**

117

Table à la Bourgogne
by J-F Oeben

How do you fit a bookcase, writing desk, travelling lap-top desk, storage space for cosmetics, and a prie-dieu all in a diminutive chest of drawers? It may seem impossible but these items are precisely what this imaginatively designed table once contained. Even though it has suffered alterations and damage since it was made, c.1760, it remains one of the rarest and most intriguing of the many multi-functional pieces produced by Jean-François Oeben, the leading ébéniste in mid-18th-century Paris (see pages 38–9).

Above **When a catch on the fourth drawer of the table à la Bourgogne is activated, four folding legs are released, allowing the drawer to operate as a lap-top writing desk for use in bed or when travelling.**

The fashion for mechanical furniture that became established in Paris in the 18th century was introduced into France through the work of German cabinet-makers such as Abraham and David Roentgen. J-F Oeben, who was likewise born in Germany, began to specialize in ingenious pieces of furniture of this kind. In order to construct the mechanisms that were required by such objects, he sought and was granted leave to build a forge in his workshop in the Arsenal district of the city. In addition to the table à la Bourgogne, Oeben developed versatile pieces that served as both desk and dressing table, one of which is believed to have graced the home of Madame de Pompadour.

The table à la Bourgogne was probably christened by Oeben as a tribute to the handicapped Duc de Bourgogne, the eldest grandson of Louis XV and elder brother of Louis XVI, for whom the cabinet-maker had invented a complicated invalid chair. In the inventory made after Oeben's death in 1763, four tables à la Bourgogne were described in detail and noted as being in various stages of completion. Only three of these are known to have survived: this example, now at Luton Hoo, was given by Jules Porges to Sir Julius Wernher; another is in the Louvre; and the third was recorded as having been sold from the private collection of the Guérault family in 1935.

At first sight the table à la Bourgogne appears to be an unremarkable five-drawered chest with a red marble top divided into two sections. But this is far from all there is to the piece. The top two "drawers" are a flap that drops forwards to

Left **An engraving of the Duc de Bourgogne, for whom J-F Oeben designed a mechanical invalid's chair. The duke lent his name to the ingenious table à la Bourgogne.**

provide a writing surface. The cavity inside (and all the drawers below) extend back only as far as the central division in the top. The top space is now bare but for a winding handle, but formerly it was probably fitted out like a writing desk, with compartments and pigeon-holes.

On the side of the desk is a small winding hole, where, if you insert the handle and turn it, a bookcase with two shelves rises as if by magic from the back, operated by a system of ratchets, gears, and weights. The vertical edges of the book-case are unusually rounded and have small curled levers at their base. Pull on these and the rounded ends rotate to display small niches containing shelves for travelling toiletries. On the shelves, porcelain pots for cream, engraved glass, and cutlery – all probably original to the piece – remain intact.

The lower drawers also contain a few surprises: the third is now empty but, as FJB Watson has pointed out, it was probably originally designed to take writing accessories. The drawer below it is much more fascinating. When you pull it out it seems to be a writing box with a tooled-leather writing surface. But beneath the base is a maze of levers, catches, and springs, and if you apply pressure to the central mechanism the drawer transforms itself into a lap-top writing desk with four curved legs that spring out automatically to support it. Presumably this would have been useful on journeys, when the user was sitting in a carriage, or wished to write in bed. The bottom drawer is now empty, but judging by its counterpart in the Louvre, it was probably originally not a drawer at all but a *prie-dieu*.

The table is veneered in Oeben's favourite later geometric style, in this case a pattern of diamonds of tulipwood with the grain running at right angles to create an effect of interlocking cubes. The handles are later replacements, probably fitted in the 19th century when other alterations were made.

The complexity of the mechanisms contained in tables of this type would have made them extremely expensive merely to be used for travelling. In fact, in the luxury-loving courts of the mid-18th century, multi-functional pieces such as this were enjoyed as much for their gimmickry as for any real practical purpose. A chest that took care of your physical, mental, and spiritual needs was a novelty that few furniture makers at the time could surpass.

Left **When the winding handle on the right-hand side of the table is turned, a tiered bookcase emerges from the back section. The rounded ends rotate and conceal shelves designed for the storage of cosmetics.**

119

Metamorphic Library Steps

The problem of how to reach the upper shelves of a large library inspired 18th-century cabinet-makers to create a remarkable array of ingenious transforming devices. The fashion for metamorphic steps – those that could be transformed into another piece of furniture – blossomed from around the middle of the century. Gradually steps evolved that turned into elegant stools, tables, chairs, or even poles. But perhaps most inventive of all was the contraption made in Bavaria that provided its fortunate owner with a library table, a chair, and a set of steps all in one.

Right **This plate from Ince and Mayhew's pattern book, *The Universal System of Household Furniture*, shows a design for a collapsible ladder-like set of library steps.**

Far right **The library at Temple Newsam, near Leeds, has a library ladder in the form of a folding pole, based on the design by Ince and Mayhew.**

Above **In central Europe in the mid-18th century library tables were often made for monastery libraries. This example, made in Bohemia, is veneered with burr walnut and inlaid with contrasting woods.**

Right **The centre of the tabletop is hinged and one section can be raised and folded back on the other to provide a very unusual set of library steps; a panel in the side pulls out and is attached to a chair with a folding back.**

The development of library steps was driven by the growing availability of books and the fashion for libraries in large houses. Until the end of the 17th century books were rarities and rarely stored in bookcases, but by the second half of the following century an extensive collection of books was an effective way to show the world how educated and refined you were. A well-stocked, comfortably furnished library was becoming a feature of most large private houses.

Cabinet-makers quickly caught up with the new trend. Ince and Mayhew, one of Britain's leading firms of furniture makers, included two designs for library steps in their pattern book *Universal System of Household Furniture* (1759–63). One of these in the Chinese style, they explained, was suited for a large room, while the other (plate xxii), of which there is an example at Temple Newsam, near Leeds, was more adaptable and ideal for confined spaces. The larger of the two designs, decorated with an elaborate web of fretwork, reflects the prevailing taste for chinoiserie. This feature also acted as a safety device in that it provided a barrier to prevent the user falling when stretching for an elusive volume. The smaller design is an intriguing, simple, yet wonderfully functional idea, consisting of a mahogany pole that could be transformed into a library ladder when needed. The ladder is made from two semi-elliptical posts with their inside flat edge hollowed out to allow the hinged rungs to fit

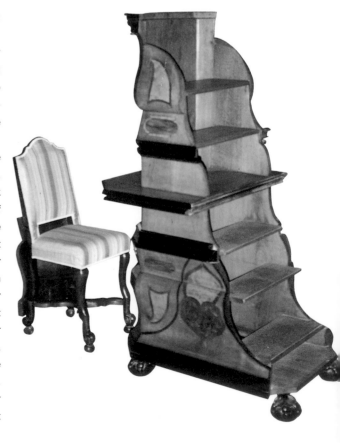

snugly inside when not in use. The user unhooked six small catches and pulled the two poles apart, causing hinged rungs to emerge, and the ladder was kept open and secure by two iron brackets. Another mid-18th-century design consisted of a long stool with six pairs of legs. When this was turned on its end, the shaped stretchers joining the legs provided steps, albeit rather steep and precarious ones.

In Bavaria and other parts of southern Germany ingenious designs were made for monastery libraries. One particularly elaborate example, unrivalled in England at that time, consists of an elaborately inlaid walnut veneered table with a solid apron standing on claw feet. One side of the piece pulls out to provide a chair with a folding backrest. The table can then be unhooked and folded back to metamorphose into a set of library steps.

Several ingenious designs emerged in 18th-century France, many of which were later adapted by English cabinet-makers. A library chair, in which the seat could be raised to reveal steps, was made by Oeben for Madame de Pompadour, while a *prie-dieu* that converted into steps was made by another *ébéniste*, P Migeon.

English cabinet-makers were not to be outdone for long, and in the later decades of the 18th century they began making increasingly sophisticated library steps. Since libraries were found only in larger houses, nearly all library steps were made from expensive timber – usually mahogany – and were finished to a very high standard. Even when made by provincial cabinet-makers they were in many cases surprisingly expensive. A bill dated 1790, for £45 for steps supplied to Earl Spencer by John King, details: "large mahogany circular library steps 9ft high with mahogany hand rails up do. and brass wires and green silk curtains in mahogany frames instead of bannisters with mahogany bookshelf and seat, the steps all carpeted with Wilton Carpet on large brass castors compleat".

At Osterley, near London, classical elegance and inventive design are combined in a carved giltwood stool and writing steps. When the steps are folded away the piece looks like a small stool, with fluted tapered legs and a classical frieze. The top of the stool lifts and hinges back, and its underside is fitted with the two lower steps, while beneath it a separate section, contained within the frieze, lifts up and can be fixed on a wooden support to form the upper section.

Meanwhile, at Harewood House, in Yorkshire, Chippendale made a set of steps in the form of a stool and decorated them with rosewood veneer and neo-classical marquetry to match the library desk he had supplied. The veneer was not nearly as sophisticated or accomplished as that decorating the desk, but the steps are nevertheless very impressive. They were operated by lifting the hinged seat, extracting the concealed steps, and locking them in place. The tall back rail prevented the user falling off and also had a narrow ledge that acted as a safety device and saved the reader the bother of climbing down before opening a heavy book.

The fashion for library steps continued apace until the early 19th century. Sheraton included designs for library steps in the form of a Pembroke table with drawers, and one of his patterns, he confessed, was inspired by a set of steps owned by the Prince of Wales (later George IV). Meanwhile, in the first decade of that century the inventive firm of Morgan & Saunders (who designed the novel globe secretaire on pages 134–5) created a Regency-style *klismos* chair that folded over to form library steps. The firm proudly described its dual-purpose chairs as "considered the best and handsomest article ever yet invented, where two complete pieces of furniture are combined in one – an elegant and truly comfortable armchair and a set of library steps". With such a piece in your library you could not only reach the elusive book on your top shelf, but read it in comfort on a fashionable seat.

Below and right **The Morgan and Saunders folding chair could be converted into library steps. The design of the chair, based on the Greek *klismos*, was very fashionable at this time.**

Right **The library steps at Harewood House, Yorkshire, were designed by Chippendale, who decorated them with classical designs to match a library desk in the same room.**

Commode Bed
by Georg Haupt

There is nothing new about hiding a bed in another piece of furniture – the idea dates back to the 17th century or even earlier – but it would be difficult to imagine a more elegant disguise for a bed than this commode. Made c.1780 by the leading Swedish cabinet-maker Georg Haupt (1741–84), this handsomely inlaid piece can be transformed into a place to sleep by pulling out the front section, which extends like a telescope. The mattress would have been kept rolled up inside and there are chunky folding legs that swing down to give the necessary extra support in the central section, and fold away when the bed is not in use.

Right **The elegant commode bed now stands in the White Cabinet, one of the most important of Gustavus III's state apartments. It was originally made not for this location but for his bedchamber.**

Far right **When the front of the commode is pulled open a telescopic bed emerges, providing a place to sleep for Gustavus III's page, who often slept in the king's bedchamber.**

Above **The Royal Palace in Stockholm was begun in the 17th century by Nicodemus Tessin the Younger, but not completed until the end of the following century.**

Right **This portrait of Gustavus III in his silver coronation robes was painted by Alexander Roslin and modelled on a famous portrait of Louis XIV.**

"Metamorphic" or transforming beds reached the peak of their popularity in the 18th century, when multi-purpose furniture was fashionable. Beds made in the form of bookcases, writing desks, cupboards, and sideboards were probably found in many well-to-do homes. The inventory made of Madame de Pompadour's possessions mentions three metamorphic beds. However, perhaps because they had so many moving parts and had to support a considerable weight, such pieces seem to have been particularly susceptible to damage, and few survive.

Georg Haupt, who made this commode bed, was the son of a Swedish cabinet-maker. Having started his apprenticeship at thirteen, he settled first in Amsterdam and then in Paris, where he is thought to have worked for the leading *ébéniste* Simon Oeben. His stay in Paris coincided with the period of gradual transition from the rococo idiom to the new classical style. As a result, classical motifs and French style were to remain a source of inspiration to Haupt throughout his career.

Haupt later set up as a cabinet-maker in London and worked with, among others, the architect William Chambers. Appointed royal cabinet-maker to King Adolf Fredrik in 1769, he returned to Stockholm, where he remained for the rest of his life.

The commode reflects Haupt's simultaneous fascination with classical forms and rococo frivolity. The urns, with their

goat's-head masks, scrolling frieze (based on the Vitruvian scroll), and laurel wreaths, are derived from antiquity, whereas the ribbons, theatrical drapery, and slightly curved legs give the commode a sense of rococo movement and light-heartedness. The "G" within the laurel wreaths on the side panels refers to Gustavus III, Adolf Fredrik's son and successor.

The bed was made for Gustavus's private bedroom in the Royal Palace in Stockholm. It was used by his life page, who by royal decree always slept at the foot of the king's bed (unless the royal couple were spending the night together) and whose duties included dressing his master every day. Despite adopting such far-reaching safety precautions, the king was unable to prevent an attempt on his life. In 1792 he was shot during a masked ball at the opera house and two weeks later died in his state bedchamber.

The private apartments were beneath Gustavus's state apartments and were redecorated soon after his accession in 1771. Before his father's death Gustavus had visited France, where he had witnessed the grandeur of Versailles and admired the sophistication of French furniture. He returned to Sweden fired with determination to re-create something of this formality, and it was Haupt, a French-trained cabinet-maker, whom he asked to supply him with suitably refined furnishings.

The overall effect of Haupt's commode is one of supreme elegance and this is helped by the extremely delicate stringing and the use of paler woods to surround the central mahogany panels. Despite the bed's stylish appearance, sleeping in it can hardly have been comfortable – it must have been like lying in a drawer. Even so, to a page tired out by many hours on duty, it must have seemed very welcoming.

French Cylinder-top Desk

A unique piece of furniture such as this is not what you would expect to win in a raffle. Yet the desk was offered as a prize in a royal lottery in 1831 and a ticket and advertisement for it was later found in one of its many secret compartments. Unusually for such an important piece, mystery has always shrouded the desk. No one knows who made it, whether its erstwhile owner bought it or received it as a gift, or how it turned up in a lottery. Nevertheless, it is an outstanding example of French craftsmanship and mechanical ingenuity.

Above **A detail of the right-hand panel on the desk's top shows one of three marquetry pictures that can be raised on stands to be admired as works of art. This one is based on an engraving by Pannini entitled** *Les Ruines du Pélopenèse.*

This highly elaborate desk, which dates from c.1777–81 and took four years to complete, was made for one of the most colourful personalities of the court of Louis XVI, the writer Caron de Beaumarchais. Today Beaumarchais is best known for *The Barber of Seville* (1775) and *The Marriage of Figaro* (1778), comic plays in which he poked fun at the aristocracy and that were later transformed into operas by Rossini and Mozart.

However, Beaumarchais was more than just a satirical dramatist. As well as being an extremely successful arms dealer, supplying the Americans with weapons during the War of Independence, he worked as a secret emissary of Louis XVI. He was also an accomplished clock maker and, it seems, equally canny when it came to choosing wives, for he twice married wealthy widows. As a result of his varied interests he had ample funds to spend on grand and expensive pieces of furniture such as this desk, for which, if the advertisement for the lottery can be believed (and there is no guarantee that it can) he paid 85,000 francs.

The top of the desk has three panels, each decorated with a marquetry picture above a frieze containing three drawers. When you open the cylinder lid you are greeted with a plethora of elaborate fittings: two compartments in the centre and three to each side. A reading slide pulls out, and in the centre is a reading stand that can be mechanically raised. On either outer side of the desk there are also smaller writing slides, which were presumably for secretarial staff to sit at.

Above **A work based on Lajoue's engraving** *l'Optique* **decorates the front of the cylinder top. It shows the sun's rays being used to ignite a fire.**

127

As a clock maker, Beaumarchais was fascinated by mechanical devices and so he must have found the complex gadgetry that this grand desk contains exactly to his taste. Many of its complex functions are controlled by the lock in the centre of the frieze. Depending on how far you insert the key and which way you turn it, you can flip open the cylinder top and the drawers of the frieze and raise the three panels on top of the desk, to admire the marquetry as pictures. The mechanism for the lock is contained within the side of the cylinder.

Inside the desk are more devices: five spring levers and catches attached to the underneath of the writing slide release secret drawers contained in the slide itself as well as the central drawer in the frieze, the slide, and its reading stand. The desk's lower section has a central drawer flanked by two deep outer drawers, one with a safe. These drawers too are mechanically operated by pressing on pads in the desk's outer wings.

Cylinder desks of this type were among the grandest and most important furnishings ever made. The form first became fashionable in the 1760s, and was probably introduced by the

ébéniste Jean-François Oeben, who was still in the process of making the Bureau du Roi (*see* pages 38–9) when he died. Therefore it is surprising that no one knows for sure who made this example. Riesener, *ébéniste* to Louis XVI, has traditionally been regarded as its maker, and is mentioned as such in the advertisement for the lottery, but recent research (by Sir Geoffrey de Bellaigue) has raised doubts about the attribution and suggests that several craftsmen were involved.

The desk is basically constructed from a pine and oak carcass. But, as you would expect in any grand piece of French furniture of this period, these modest indigenous woods were smothered with elaborate gilt-bronze mounts and marquetry panels. The mounts on the legs are extraordinarily lavish, cast as mermaid caryatids. The marquetry is designed as a series of *trompe-l'oeil* pictures that are "framed" by their surrounding veneer: tulipwood, purple-wood, mahogany, sycamore, holly, box, and ebony are among an enormous range of woods used to create them. Today, faded by sunlight and the patina of age,

Above **The mermaid caryatid supports at each corner of the desk may refer to the success of Beaumarchais in breaching English naval blockades to supply arms to America.**

the marquetry pictures are still awe-inspiring in their complexity, but when they were first made the woods would have had none of the present softness of tone and would have appeared as brilliantly coloured as a painted canvas. One can only imagine how eye-catching they must have been.

All the decorative motifs seem to have been selected with an eye to Beaumarchais' various interests and achievements. Scenes that illustrate the sciences of optics and astronomy decorate the front and back. These refer perhaps to the owner's interest in science and the mechanical arts that flourished in the age of enlightenment. The panels adorned with classical ruins reflect the prevailing fascination with classical antiquity as well as Beaumarchais' taste in art. He is known to have found such subjects especially pleasing, and owned several canvases of architectural *capriccios* by the celebrated artists Hubert Robert and G. Pannini.

Many of the more complex marquetry compositions were based on contemporary engravings that were adapted to suit the desk, but the still lifes of fruit and flowers that decorate the lower section of the desk have no known prototypes and were probably specially commissioned for the piece. When the styles of marquetry used on the upper panels are compared with those below, it is clear that while the architectural and scientific scenes above depict intricate details and light and shade by the use of staining and hatching (inscribing) on to the various veneers, the still lifes below rely on shading (probably achieved by dipping the pieces of wood into hot sand) and by using wood of varying colours, to create the effect of light and shadow. These distinctive differences in style have led Sir Geoffrey de Bellaigue to suggest that several craftsmen were involved in making the marquetry panels.

In contrast to the somewhat academic subject matter that decorates the upper part of the desk, the decoration on the inside is pure whimsy. Playing cards, a set of dividers, a pen, a book, and a pamphlet written by Beaumarchais himself lie casually discarded. It is not hard to imagine that their owner has just left the room and might return at any moment to solve the mystery of his desk.

Above **Marquetry panels with the subject of fruit and flowers decorate the desk's lower section. The techniques used here differ markedly from those in the upper panels, and this suggests that the two sets of panels were created by different craftsmen.**

Right **The Beaumarchais desk is seen here in Baron Ferdinand de Rothschild's sitting room at Waddesdon Manor. The marquetry that decorates the writing slide includes political pamphlets by Beaumarchais on the American War of Independence.**

Mechanical Table by Martin Carlin

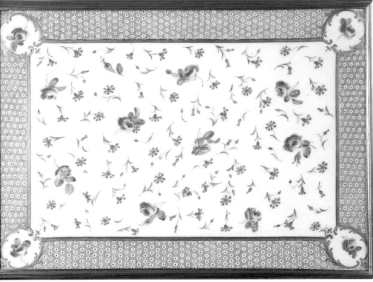

Martin Carlin's jewel-like furniture was ideally suited to grace the salons of fashionable boudoirs and salons of the mid to late 18th century. Madame du Barry and Mademoiselle Laguerre, who were both wealthy mistresses, were among the admirers of his work, as were many members of the French royal family, including Marie Antoinette. This writing table, made c.1781 and decorated with exquisite Sèvres porcelain plaques and sumptuous gilt-metal mounts, typifies the luxurious furniture for which the ébéniste was celebrated.

Above **Characteristically richly coloured, exquisitely painted, and lavishly gilded, the Sèvres plaques decorating the top and sides of the table are made from soft paste porcelain, which at this time was made concurrently with hard paste.**

Right **The table's simple shape and small size are typical of Carlin's work. The mounts are set against backgrounds of varnished metal, while the legs are inset with brass, creating a fluted effect.**

During the third quarter of the 18th century Martin Carlin (c.1730–85) was Paris's leading maker of porcelain-mounted furniture. Commodes, secretaires, tables and jewel cabinets were among some eighty pieces of porcelain-mounted furniture that he is recorded as having made. All Carlin's furniture was commissioned by the *marchand-merciers* (furniture retailers) Philippe Poirier and Dominique Daguerre (for whom this was made), then usually displayed in their showrooms before being sold to their illustrious clientele (*see* also pages 104–5). Although precisely who was responsible for designing such complex and lavishly decorated pieces remains questionable, it seems likely that the elegant design was probably largely due to the *marchand-merciers*, who had a virtual monopoly on the supply of Sèvres plaques. Some inspiration for the mechanism within the table may also have come from a table made by Riesener for Marie Antoinette. This had a top that contained a book rest that could be raised for reading when standing.

At the time this table was made the Sèvres factory was enjoying great popularity, producing porcelain of unequalled splendour. The factory had been nurtured by France's royal family. Louis XV had saved from extinction the predecessor of Sèvres, the Vincennes factory (which was started by one of his civil servants) by lending financial assistance. Louis later moved the factory to Sèvres, which was conveniently close to his palace at Versailles and not far from the home of his influential mistress, Madame Pompadour. Louis XVI, on his accession to

Right **The table's top can be propped up to support a book, while the whole surface can be raised telescopically to allow the user to read comfortably in a standing position.**

the throne, retained control of the factory, thus ensuring the continuing cachet of its expensive products.

The nine soft paste porcelain plaques with which this piece is decorated are characteristic of the delicacy and style of Sèvres porcelain of this date. Each plaque is scattered with sprigs of roses and cornflowers on a white ground and framed by a distinctive border, sometimes described as *oeil de perdrix* (partridge eye), created by a series of small dots around a series of white reserves.

In the fashion-conscious boudoirs of Paris elegant, multi-functional tables of this type must have enjoyed considerable success. Two other tables of similar design and quality are in the Huntington Art Gallery, California and the Wallace Collection, London. The one in the latter collection may have once belonged to Queen Marie Antoinette. Martin Carlin also made a number of tables that had less elaborate mechanisms and were decorated with lacquer panels instead of porcelain plaques.

The table is made from an oak carcass veneered with sycamore and maple and decorated with gilt bronze mounts. In its closed position it is designed to be the right height for sitting and reading or writing. The ingenious design meant that the drawers did not have to be opened manually. The top one jumps out at the turn of the key in the frieze because, behind the drawer, a steel spring that is fixed to the back of the case pushes it out when released. Inside, the drawer is fitted as a miniature desk: on one side are compartments for ink, sponge, and pounce (powder to dry the ink). On the other is a larger compartment for paper, topped with a leather-lined writing slide. The deeper drawer below, designed for storage, pops open in a similar way at the press of a catch behind the front.

131

The mechanism also allowed a book to be supported while the user was writing. Pressing a knob at the back releases another spring, automatically lifting the top, which can then be supported on a bracket. If one wanted to read to a gathering of friends the whole top could be raised to a comfortable standing height before holding forth. There are brass pillars hidden in the stiles (vertical corner supports), which are interconnected by means of a system of cogs, pinions, and an axle, so that the top would support itself and remain level at whatever height was required. As the evening drew in and the light dimmed, one could also pull out slides from each side of the table to take candlesticks to illuminate the book.

The top of the table is made from two thicknesses of wood pivoted together with a central bolt. This construction allows anyone reading to an assembly to swivel the top so as to face and specifically address a person or a group of people not directly in front of the reader. Even if the audience were not impressed by the literary skills on display, they must have been by the versatile design of Carlin's versatile table.

Mechanical Desk by Giovanni Socci

Probably the ultimate in ingenious writing furniture, this mechanical desk was made by the Florentine furniture maker Giovanni Socci (fl.1807–39). It combines desk and seat in a single piece but when closed it looks just like an elegant oval commode. The piece is made from richly figured mahogany with simple gilt metal mounts and a marble top, and the rather severe outline and restrained decoration are characteristic of the Empire style, which became synonymous with the rule of Napoleon Bonaparte.

Above **Giovanni Socci's mechanical desk is now housed in the Salle Elisa at the château of Fontainebleau, where it is appropriately surrounded by other French Empire-style furniture.**

The central "drawers" of this innovative desk are dummy fronts that form the back of the chair, and when you pull them the chair emerges on a sliding platform. The seat is upholstered in red leather and supported on three legs. The two legs at the back of the piece are in the outward-curving sabre style, which was derived from the ancient Greek *klismos* chair and, at this time, the epitome of the Empire style. When the chair is pulled out the central leg has to slide through a groove in the main central platform and so is of a simpler turned shape than the other two. The marble top is made in two halves, which part to reveal a leather-covered writing slope and a small writing box that pops up and takes stationery, ink, and pens.

Giovanni Socci was one of the leading early-19th-century cabinet-makers to introduce the Empire style to Italy. When Napoleon's sister Elisa Bacciochi was promoted to the position of Grand Duchess of Tuscany in 1808, she moved into and renovated the Pitti Palace in Florence, and Socci was on hand to supply her with suitably modern furniture. Elisa, born in Ajaccio, Corsica in 1777, had longed for a role in Napoleon's expanding Empire and in 1805 had been made responsible for the Italian principality of Lucca. In that capacity she expanded the local industry, doubling silk production and developing the marble quarries at Carrara (on the brink of collapse because of poor management), and opened libraries, schools, and hospitals.

Socci made three or four desks of this type. All of these were believed to have been made for Eliza, who had a great

Left **Pietro Benvenuti painted this portrait of Elisa Bacciochi and her daughter, whom she christened Napoléone in honour of her brother, Napoleon I (whose bust stands on the table). The view of Florence glimpsed through the open window refers to Elisa's status as Grand Duchess of Tuscany.**

interest in the Arts, when she took up residence in the Pitti Palace (two are still there). However, since one of the pieces is dated 1807, the year before she took over the Pitti, the first model may well have been made for Elisa's predecessor, the Queen Regent Marie Louise de Bourbon.

The example shown here, which is now at Fontainebleau, was for many years part of the collection of furniture on display at the Château de Malmaison (*see* also Empress Josephine's Bed, pages 68–71) and was always said to have been a gift from Elisa to Napoleon, whom she adored.

However, recent research suggests that Elisa did not give the desk to her brother but that it belonged to her and she took it with her when she fled from Florence and went into exile on Napoleon's fall from grace. After Elisa's death the piece passed to her equally strong-willed daughter, Napoléone, then, on her death in 1869, into the collection of Napoleon III, and from there to the French National Collections.

Above **The mechanical desk is seen here in the open position. When the desk is closed the writing slide, stationery compartment, and the chair on its plinth retract and the piece looks like an oval commode.**

Globe Secretaire

This piece appears strange from the outside – rather like a giant segmented orange – but it conceals a no less unusual interior. The upper part has two quadrant-shaped doors that unfold to reveal a hidden writing desk. Supported on a single hinge in the lower corner, the doors give the illusion of great fragility, almost like a butterfly's wing. This globe secretaire was based on a pattern called the Pitt's Cabinet Globe Writing Table, invented by George Remington in the early 19th century and made by Morgan & Sanders.

Right **This novel piece, when opened, was intended to attract attention rather than serve any practical function. The drawers in the interior are veneered in satinwood, creating a contrast with the rich mahogany exterior.**

Far right **Ebony inlay and heavy gilt-bronze metal mounts add richness and visual interest to the simple shape when closed.**

Above **This advertisement for the cabinet-makers Morgan & Sanders was published in Ackermann's *Repository of the Arts* in 1810 and illustrated various designs for globe writing tables. Similar secretaires were also made on the Continent.**

Right **The home of the Wernher family from 1903, Luton Hoo in Bedfordshire was built in the 18th century by Robert Adam, who described the house as his most impressive "both in point of elegance and contrivance".**

Although its undeniably bizarre design was its main attraction, the piece could function as a desk if necessary. The doors and the central part of the hemisphere are fitted out with a mixture of drawers and pigeon-holes, while in the lower hemisphere there are yet more surprises. A hinged reading and writing slide can be pulled forward and raised, and below it is a green baize-lined well. However, practicality was never a principal consideration for the owner of this type of furniture. If you were a wealthy Regency aristocrat, the globe writing table would have provided you with a conversation piece for your library, something with which to intrigue your friends as you showed off your impressive collection of books after dinner.

The piece was made c.1810 by the leading firm of cabinet-makers Morgan & Sanders, who supplied furniture to prominent figures of the day, including members of the royal family and Lord Nelson. Among their specialities was multi-purpose and novelty furniture that could transform itself from one shape and function to another – for example, chairs that could be turned upside down to serve as library steps. Realizing the potential of the idea, the makers advertised the desk as "an indispensable appendage to the library of every person of taste in the fashionable world". A library was a room that only the wealthy would enjoy and therefore, like most library furniture of the day, this is a high-quality piece in which the use of fashionable expensive woods signals its prestige. The outer shell is veneered in richly figured mahogany. Inside, the drawers are

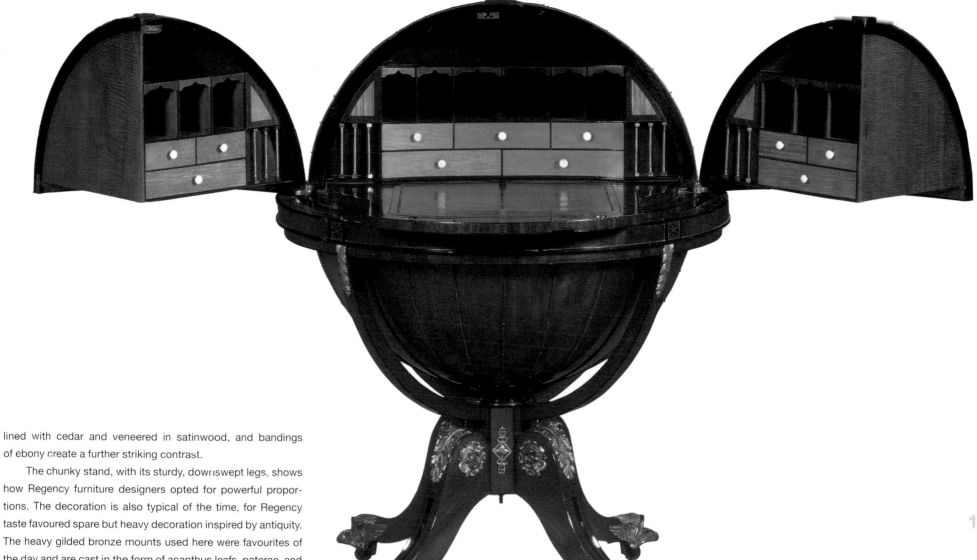

lined with cedar and veneered in satinwood, and bandings of ebony create a further striking contrast.

The chunky stand, with its sturdy, downswept legs, shows how Regency furniture designers opted for powerful proportions. The decoration is also typical of the time, for Regency taste favoured spare but heavy decoration inspired by antiquity. The heavy gilded bronze mounts used here were favourites of the day and are cast in the form of acanthus leafs, paterae, and winged claw feet. Sadly, despite both the effusive claims of the advertisement and the care that went into the quirky design, the idea appears not to have caught on. In consequence, this is one of very few such desks and is therefore a great rarity.

The inspiration for Morgan & Sanders' unusual desk may have come from the continent, where globe desks and work tables of similar shape were made in the fashionable Biedermeier style. Josef Danhauser, a celebrated Viennese cabinet-maker, made similar pieces. However, the proportions of the Continental versions are invariably much less impressive (this exceptionally large version of the form measures 3ft 10in (117cm) in height and 2ft 11in (89cm) in diameter) and the pieces are less elaborately finished.

Morgan & Sanders named their innovative design the Pitt's Cabinet Globe Writing Table after William Pitt the Younger, the celebrated Tory politician. Pitt had died in 1806, two years before Morgan & Sanders acquired the manufacturing rights to make these desks from their inventor, George Remington, and

the firm must have hoped that naming the desk after England's youngest-ever prime minister would give it added cachet.

This piece was until recently one of the treasures of Luton Hoo, home of the Wernher family, and was bought by Sir Harold Wernher. The son of Sir Julius Wernher, a self-made diamond magnate who became influential in both royal and political circles, Sir Harold had a shrewd business sense and a great love of beauty. He married the exotic Lady Zia, a descendant of Tsar Nicholas I and granddaughter of Pushkin, and having returned to Luton Hoo after the Second World War, expanded the family collection of English furniture. This is one of the remarkable pieces from the outstanding collection he acquired at that time, which includes the table à la Bourgogne (*see* pages 118–19).

Castle
Dining Table

This must rank as one of the most unusual, indeed eccentric, tables ever made. The piece has an impressive six-sided parquetry top and a base whose odd, three-dimensional decoration is intended to simulate bricks. The purpose of the "brickwork" is suddenly revealed when the table is closed and transforms itself into a miniature castle. Presumably the idea was that when it was not in conventional use the piece would function as a talking point in any room, while the flat inner lid could provide a stand for decorative objects.

Above **When it is dismantled the table reveals a total of eleven component parts plus the base. Each of these must be slotted together with the other parts to form either the castle or the table.**

Right **In its open state as a table, the boldly patterned parquetry top creates a striking impact that is effectively balanced by the sturdy base of the castle.**

The table is converted into a castle by first unclipping the four triangular panels, which can then be lifted away from the base. The four square panels, each supported by metal stays, also slide out. A square beech frame is then fitted over the trunk of the table and the square panels are slotted back in an upright position, with their outer surfaces now visible. A separate top, made in imitation of a castle parapet with crenellations, and rustic corbels and inlaid with parquetry on its inner surface, holds the top of the four square panels in place.

Although the design is intriguing, the piece is of simple construction and was produced using basic techniques. It was perhaps made by an inventive provincial cabinet-maker who was more interested in the design's overall impact than in painstaking craftsmanship. It is constructed entirely from indigenous country woods: box, beech, fruitwood, pine, poplar, and walnut. The top is veneered with three simple parquetry designs each using the same three woods: box, walnut, and fruitwood, and the overall effect creates a highly effective patchwork of colour and pattern. The veneers are thickly cut – another sign of simple rural woodworking techniques – and are laid on to thickly cut panels of poplar that were originally painted on the reverse, perhaps to ward off attack from predatory woodworm. Likewise, the base is simple, with a boarded pine carcass on to which have been applied the cherry plinth and three-dimensional bricks that form the façade above.

Despite the table's simplicity, the maker took considerable care with details such as the panelled door and the shuttered windows on the upper storey and with the wedge-shaped stones (*voussoirs*) forming the arched openings for windows and doors. On the upper folding storey, the façade simulates brickwork by using alternating veneers of fruitwood and beech, cut into small rectangles, and the design is linked to that of the base by the use of three-dimensional wooden bricks to create quoining on the corners and around the window frame.

So unusual is this piece that its precise origins and age are hard to pinpoint, and expert opinion remains divided. The choice of woods, octagonal top, simplicity of construction, and the antiquarian castle design suggest that it was probably made in the second quarter of the 19th century, possibly in the vicinity of Munich or in northern Italy. However, this piece is so unique that, in the absence of documentary evidence, it is difficult to say where or why it was made. But whoever the craftsman was, and whatever his motivation, we can hardly fail to be beguiled by his whimsical creation.

Right **When this ingenious piece was closed, to present a castle complete with detailed brickwork, barred windows, and crenellations, it must have served as a novel talking point, whatever the setting in which it once stood.**

137

Mechanical Table by Robert Jupe

Above **This William IV mahogany extending capstan table was made by Robert Jupe c.1835.**

Among the novel forms of dining table that evolved during the early decades of the 19th century, Robert Jupe's patent table is hard to beat for sheer ingenuity. Jupe discovered a way to extend a circular table from the centre by means of an innovative capstan, and patented his design in 1835. Such was the success of this novel concept that the table, with various forms of pedestal support, continued to be made throughout the 19th century and has recently inspired an inventive modern-day counterpart (see pages 140–1).

Right **Extended before extra leaves have been inserted, the table shows Jupe's ingenuity. Metal supports push the leaves out along wooden runners.**

Below **The diagram prepared by Jupe for his patent was one of several he submitted on 11 March 1835. Circular extending tables came in three sizes and he also designed rectangular and oval versions.**

The fashion for extending tables enjoyed its heyday during the 19th century in Britain. Throughout this period a rapidly growing affluent population living in houses with rooms of limited size created a ready market for practical, adaptable furniture. There emerged a wide range of expanding tables, and these operated in a variety of ways. In 1800 Richard Gillow patented an expanding table that was operated by "attaching to a table mounted upon a frame and legs … wooden or metal sliders, which run on dovetail, T or square or cylindrical or other grooves with or without wheels or rollers". Three years later Sheraton commented of dining tables: "there are various sorts now in use, and some under the protection of His Majesty's patent. The common useful dining-tables are upon pillar and claws … A dining-table of this kind may be made to any size, by having a sufficient quantity of pillars and claw parts, for between each of them is a loose flap, fixed by means of iron straps and buttons, so that they are easily taken off and put aside."

Other alternatives included the Cumberland-action table, which contained extra leaves and legs within a narrow apron under the top; tables that were extended with a winding handle; and examples with a central pillar that could split in two, so that extra leaves could be slotted into place. Circular dining tables were ideally suited to less generously proportioned rooms, but their drawback was that they were more difficult to extend than rectangular or oval tables, in which it was easy enough to insert one or two extra leaves to make the table top bigger.

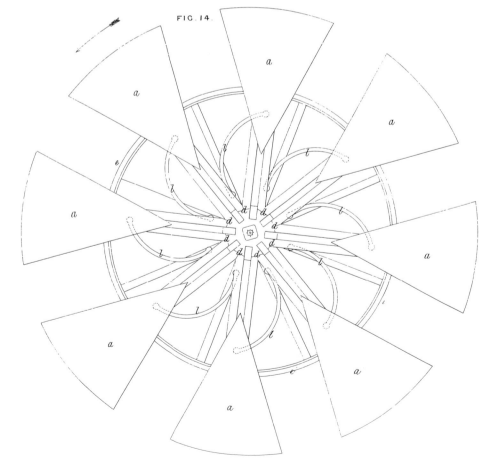

FIG. 14.

Jupe shrewdly solved this problem by designing a table in which the circular top was cut into six or eight segments, held underneath on a spoked, cartwheel-like framework of wooden rails. In the middle, what looked like a simple pedestal support was in fact a capstan – a rotating barrel. When you turned the top of the table, the capstan pushed out banana-shaped cast-iron ribs which were attached to the segmented leaves. As you rotated the top, the segments slid outwards along the wooden rails, like a flower opening its petals. Then the gaps between the segments could be filled with six or eight extra leaves.

The tables came in various dimensions, and some of the grander versions, such as this, had two sets of leaves, allowing you to vary the amount by which you increased the size. The diameter of this example was 70in (178cm) without leaves, 84in (213cm) with small leaves, and 100in (254cm) with large ones.

Jupe's tables were usually made from solid rich red mahogany, and the purchaser was supplied with a handsome mahogany box in which the extra leaves could be stored when they were not in use. The tables were constructed with various simple but appropriate legs. Some have a flat, four-legged plinth with claw feet; others have cabriole or scrolled supports. The claw feet and flat, four-branched base that support this table are simpler than some more heavily carved examples.

Jupe's clever patent also included designs for an oval and a rectangular dining table that operated on the same principle. It is a great testimony to both the success of his design and the quality of his craftsmanship that so many Jupe tables survive in good working condition, and in consequence their value has rocketed in recent decades.

However, despite his relatively new-found fame, little is known of Jupe's career. He was part of a company called John Johnstone, Jupe & Co, based in New Bond Street from c.1835 to c.1839, and then set up on his own in Welbeck Street, while John Johnstone went on to form a new partnership with Jeanes operating from the same premises. As well as his handsomely designed tables, Jupe is also known to have made wardrobes.

A well-liked and much-respected maker, he nevertheless guarded his table design jealously, although his former partner must have had some claim to the patented design since an example stamped Johnstone & Jeanes Patent recently passed through the salerooms. In 1836 Jupe is recorded as having brought a case against a certain Mr Pratt, whom he accused of infringement of his patented design. An impressive array of well-known furniture makers turned up in the courtroom to lend support to Jupe, including Edward Bailey of Bailey & Saunders, furniture makers to George IV. Pratt argued that there was no infringement because Jupe had copied the idea from Gillows, a prominent furniture-making firm who had invented a telescopic dining table. The judge noted that "in the last 10 or 12 years it has been the fashion to dine at a round table" and, having weighed the evidence, supported Jupe and decided against the unfortunate Pratt. "I have seen Jupe's table, in my judgment it is entirely new; I consider it decidedly better than Gillow's table. I am of the opinion that Pratt's is on the same principle."

Mechanical Table by Senior Carmichael

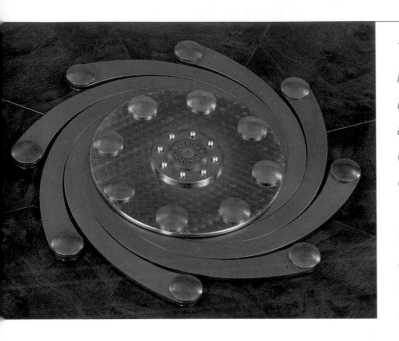

To create this innovative table, the leading furniture designer-makers Senior Carmichael took the fascinating mechanics of Robert Jupe's extending capstan table (see pages 138–9) and refined, modernized, and literally turned them upside down. In punning acknowledgement of the 19th-century craftsman's role in inspiring the design, the piece is entitled "Jepu Balet (anag, 4,5)". To date the progressive two-man team have made two tables to this ingenious design. One, made of English oak, is with the Smallpiece Trust, a charity that promotes education in design; the one seen here, made of burr walnut, is in a private collection in Switzerland.

Right **The table top is veneered with American black burr walnut, a distinctive, richly figured timber that was chosen to complement the metal mechanism in the centre. The underframe is made from solid American black walnut, with details made from bubinga, a deep-red hardwood.**

Above **The central capstan, made from engine-turned steel, provides the design's decorative focal point as well as containing its mechanics.**

Right **The caps at the end of each of the bronze arms can be removed in order to allow candleholders to be attached.**

Charles Wheeler Carmichael and Rupert Senior were contemporaries of mine at John Makepeace's School for Craftsmen in Wood at Parnham House, and afterwards I shared my first two workshops with them. This expanding circular table is one of the most widely acclaimed designs by this partnership, which operates from workshops in Surrey. The patented table has been exhibited at the New York International Contemporary Furniture Fair and in an exhibition entitled "Decorative Arts Today" at Bonham's, in Knightsbridge, London. It has been awarded a guild mark by the Worshipful Company of Furniture Makers and its designers were finalists in the Prince Philip Prize for designer of the year.

But what led Senior Carmichael to rethink the original design? The fact is that while they admired Jupe's concept, they felt that much of his table's charm was hidden beneath the top. Unless you see it in action or know how it works, it looks just like an ordinary circular table. However, by placing the mechanism on the table's top, Senior Carmichael fused form and function. Moreover, when they are visible the moving parts also serve to decorate the piece.

The table operates on much the same principle as Jupe's patented design. The top is divided into segments that fit together with tongue-and-groove joints. Rotating the top

causes the curved metal arms to unfurl, pushing the wooden segments to which they are attached outwards along runners hidden under the top and leaving spaces in between for the insertion of additional leaves. Fully extended, the table seats twelve, while in compacted form it is suitable for six. When they are not in use the spare leaves can be stored in a separate carousel that also provides a candlestand.

In a table designed by Jupe the working parts were crudely made from iron and the expanding arms took up nearly the whole of the underside of the piece. Before they could transfer the mechanism to the top of the table, Senior Carmichael had to refine it and reduce its size, so that it would look attractive and take up only the central area, allowing most of the surface to be used for dining. The result was a precision-made device "with the quality of a watch movement" that turns and expands smoothly and easily.

The sophisticated finish of the mechanism adds greatly to the table's visual appeal. Engine-turned stainless steel is used for the central disc, and the arms are made from patinated bronze. The mechanical hub is echoed in the design of the base, and the curved wooden elements that form the legs are punctuated with circular motifs intended to look like rivets and mirror those on the top. Similar discs of wood decorate the base and form the feet. The bulbous, rivet-like ends of the metal arms are caps that can be removed and replaced with candleholders. The reason for this feature, its designers explain, is that the table is seen at its best when flickering candles highlight the metallic tones of bronzed steel. The Swiss owner of the burr walnut table reports that it is almost universally admired by those who see it and that he still greatly enjoys using it – proof that this inventive design is also an effective one.

Compared with Jupe's capstan table, this is a streamlined 20th-century design with minimal extraneous ornament and certainly none of the carved decorative detailing, animals' paws, and gilding so admired a century ago. Tailor-made for the modern dining room, the table perfectly illustrates how the designs of past centuries may be reinterpreted and modified to provide distinctive furniture that is no less visually appealing or functional – merely different.

Folly
Keepsake Boxes

Follies were small ornamental buildings used to create an interesting focal point or a concealed novelty in a garden or park. Popular during the 18th and 19th centuries, they were built in a wide range of architectural styles, reflecting growing interest in garden design and appreciation of classical, romantic, or picturesque landscapes. When David Linley Furniture was commissioned by Alfred Dunhill to create a series of gentleman's keepsake boxes, taking architectural follies as a theme seemed to present the perfect opportunity to create an imaginative series of pieces each full of intricate detail and unusual features.

Right **The Pavilion opens to reveal a series of partitioned trays for storing keepsakes. A secret drawer in the plinth can be released only by pressing the drawer.**

Far right **The use of contrasting burr woods to create the façade of the Gothic Fort makes the building appear to be lit by candles from within.**

Above **A folly based on a classical temple built for Lord Burlington in the gardens of Chiswick House is seen here in a painting by Pieter Andreas Rysbrack (1690–1748).**

Right **The striking domed design of the sycamore and cherry-wood Pavilion was inspired by a folly that was built in the 18th century for the Earl of Kent.**

We embarked on this commission having already successfully designed for the same client a series of architectural humidors inspired by the designs of famous architects. We decided therefore to continue the architectural theme, creating a link between the two commissions. Follies, we decided, provided rich architectural subject-matter on which to draw.

One of the most difficult things about the challenge was to create designs that would be similar enough to look as if they were part of a series and yet would be stylistically distinctive from one another. Before we arrived at our final selection of five follies our design team devised about ten boxes and then, by gradual elimination, selected those that seemed as different as possible from one another.

Choosing woods of distinctive colour and grain for each box also played an important role in giving each an individual appearance. The three main woods we chose are those we always use: oak, walnut, and sycamore, but to create depth, colour, illusion, and variety we also used a palette of more exotic veneers in much the same way that an artist builds up an image with paint. All five boxes display a wide range of woodworking techniques. Architectural elements are portrayed both three-dimensionally, with turned columns, balustrades, and crisply cut steps and crenellations; and two-dimensionally, using inlays

to define mouldings, tracery, and the panelling on doors. Each of the five boxes is loosely based on the features of a particular architectural style rather than on any single building.

The Lodge draws on Renaissance architecture, with a high, marquetry balustraded loggia and a turned balustraded parapet above topped with turned finials. The main wood, sycamore, is pale and indistinctly grained, and is effectively contrasted with the richly coloured vavona burr used for the distinctive lower storey, which contains a secret compartment that can only be opened by pressing inwards on the panel in the correct spot. As with each of the boxes, the main storage space is incorporated at the top. The hinged lid is backed by a mirror and when opened reveals a compartment that, in this case, is divided into three layers. As you lift each tray out of the central space another appears before you, and the boxes are so perfectly constructed that when you replace the trays they float gently down on a cushion of air.

The Fort, which was inspired by Gothic architecture, is principally made of walnut with madrone burr and inlays of burr ash and walnut. The windows are decorated with intersected tracery, depicted in marquetry with a golden burr-ash inlay, that makes the building look as if it is lit by candles from within. The octagonal form is emphasized by the distinctive stepped walnut plinth on which the structure is placed. The lid opens to reveal two layers of storage space, a compartment is hidden in the

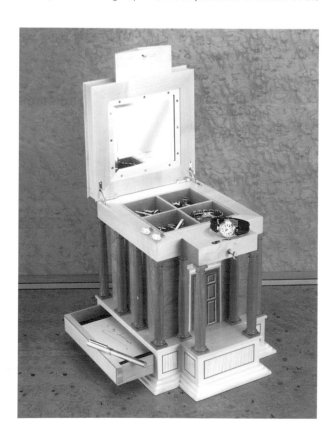

143

middle storey, and the bottom façade can be pulled forward to reveal yet another concealed storage space.

One of the most sculptural of the boxes, the Pavilion has a sycamore dome and hand-turned cherry-wood columns on a plinth of sycamore. The fielded panelled door looks three-dimensional as if carved, but is in fact *trompe-l'oeil* marquetry. The domed lid lifts up and contains its main storage area, and there is a concealed compartment in the side of the plinth.

The Villa is based on neoclassical follies and made mainly from walnut inlaid with satinwood. Solid hand-turned maple columns and a minutely detailed balustrade create a strong contrast with the deeply coloured primary wood, while the golden satinwood-inlaid windows create the same effect of candlelit glow as used on the Fort.

Finally, the Tower has a Gothic octagonal turret attached to the main structure, concealing an ingenious secret storage

Left **The sycamore arches of the Lodge are filled with veneers of bird's-eye maple and a contrasting balustrade of vavona burr. Each of the minute finials and columns on the parapet was painstakingly turned by hand.**

Below **Our final watercolour for the Tower. The asymmetrical design allows the octagonal turret's top to be lifted out to reveal tiered storage trays, while the main building's hinged roof has compartments for storing larger items.**

144

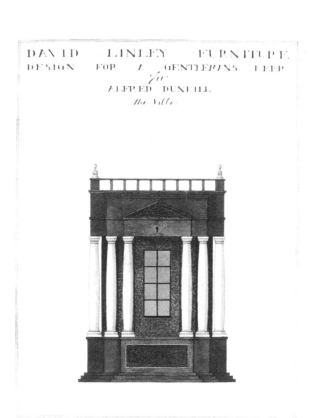

compartment: the top lifts off and underneath it are layered octagonal storage trays linked by a central support. The primary wood, English burr oak, is interspersed with intricate inlaid details made from Swiss pear, walnut, burr oak, and harewood. Sharply defined crenellations are cut from solid oak, as is the stepped plinth on which the building stands, and the door is veneered in brown oak cut across the grain in strips to create a herringbone effect.

A true folly performed no practical function, since it was conceived and built purely to delight the eye. Our folly boxes may break with tradition in that they are designed to be useful, but in their variety, craftsmanship, and ingenuity they provide their owners with small-scale visual pleasure – in much the same way that architectural follies have done in gardens throughout the centuries.

Above **The square structure of the Villa, seen here as a watercolour, was softened by the use of projecting plinths on each of its sides. The intention of this design was to reflect the harmonious elegance and the symmetry that are typical of neoclassical follies.**

Right **Three-dimensional detail and inlay are combined to decorate the Villa's graceful walnut façade. The other woods that were used, which include maple for the columns and satinwood for the windows, were selected for their contrasting colour and grain.**

145

Extraordinary Alternatives
furniture of eccentric design and unusual materials

Pieces of furniture produced from or incorporating glass, horn, metal, paper, and other unconventional materials are among the most obviously "extraordinary" ever made. But unusual ingredients are not necessarily a prerequisite for quirky design: wood has proved a versatile medium for the creation of some notable eccentricities. On the following pages the work of well-known international designers is seen beside the imaginative legacy of unidentified craftsmen.

Left **These three panels form part of a six-panel screen, shown below, that is located at Waddesdon Manor, in Buckinghamshire. Made in the early 18th century and based on designs by Desportes, the screen is covered with finely knotted Savonnerie panels, each of which shows different birds and animals.**

Walnut and Stumpwork Cabinet

Bedecked with richly coloured needlework panels, this fine cabinet on stand remains as unfaded and colourful as it must have been when made, c.1670. It represents an unusual collaboration between the cabinet-maker who created the exquisitely veneered framework and outer doors and the skilful needlewoman whose painstakingly stitched panels adorn the interior. Cabinets originated on the European mainland and this one is interesting as an early example of English craftmen's assimilation of a newly fashionable form.

Right **The largest panel lines the inside of the cabinet's lid and depicts Salome showing the head of John the Baptist to King Herod. Many of these figures, birds, and other decorative details would have been copied from pattern books that were widely available at the time.**

Above (top) **Inside the cabinet, bright embroidery and richly figured walnut veneers create a jewel-like effect.**

Above **The doors are lined with embroidered panels that portray Charles II and Queen Catherine of Braganza.**

Right **The marquetry on the outer doors was a decorative technique fashionable in England after the Restoration.**

Needlework was long an essential part of the education of well-to-do young ladies, and during the 17th century the routine method of teaching a girl to embroider comprised several distinct stages. First she would learn basic techniques on a white-work sampler, then move on to a coloured sampler, and finally, if she was really proficient, she would try her hand at raised work (a technique known as stumpwork after the 19th century). Unlike the many embroidered textiles that served a practical purpose, raised work was used purely as decoration since it was too fragile to be functional.

The technique consisted of embroidering the figurative designs using a variety of stitches, and highlighting certain elements within a design by creating a raised effect. Various unusual ingredients were incorporated to provide these areas of low relief. In this example wooden moulds covered in silk have been used for the hands and faces of figures. Additional decorative elements, such as the birds, flowers, and trees, are worked in a thick thread that is in fact a strand of metal wrapped in silk and known as purl. The wreaths surrounding the portraits lining the doors are created from a series of loops of parchment covered in silk and the textured effect is made even more impressive by a scattering of seed pearls and coral beads.

A hotch-potch of biblical and mythological scenes and royal portraits was typical subject-matter in this type of embroidery. Here Charles II and Queen Catherine of Braganza appear on the inside of the doors; the lid is lined with a depiction of Salome

presenting John the Baptist's head to Herod; and a central panel shows the Finding of Moses. The drawers above show pastoral scenes on either side of a small panel embroidered with the arms of the Haynes family, for whom the cabinet was made. The four middle drawers depict the four elements; those below show the Rape of Europa and Narcissus at the fountain.

One of the most appealing characteristics of these designs is the naïve randomness of scale in each picture. For example, in the scene depicting Salome presenting the head of John the Baptist to Herod, the flowers and fruits that are used to fill in the background are massive compared with the central figures. Such discrepancies are partly due to the fact that many of the decorative elements employed in embroidery were copied directly, with little regard to overall scale, from popular pattern books such as the *Second Book of Flowers, Fruits, Beastes, Birds and Flies Exactly Drawn*.

In its style and in the internal arrangement of doors and drawers, the cabinet follows fashions established in northern Europe and Italy, where cabinets were fashionable long before they were widely sought after in England. The exterior is veneered with oysters of walnut and the doors are inlaid with oval marquetry panels that are filled with arabesques of sycamore, walnut, and ebony. At 52in (132cm) the cabinet is not tall, perhaps to allow easy access to the top, which was used as a storage space for jewels and has a hinged lid that can be raised to reveal an interior lined with its original pink silk.

Inside the cabinet, the embroidery panels are surrounded with richly coloured concave walnut mouldings, providing a frame for each picture that allows you to admire every scene both as an individual work of art and as part of an overall scheme. The interior cupboard door opens to disclose a cavity fitted with an arcade of gilded columns and angled mirrors that conceal secret compartments. The stand is supported by six barley-twist legs joined by an elaborately shaped stretcher; these, although stylistically in keeping with the date of the piece, are later replacements.

The cabinet was made for a member of the Haynes family, who lived in Copford Hall, Essex. John Haynes (d.1674) was Connecticut's first Governor and it may have been produced for his son or grandson, and perhaps embroidered by one of the ladies of the family. The piece remained in the Haynes family until the early years of this century, when it came on to the open market. From 1920 until recently it was at Groombridge Place in Kent, where, surrounded by a notable collection of Charles II furniture, it was so perfectly at home in one of England's most famous Restoration houses that it became known as "The Groombridge Cabinet". After reappearing on the market it is now in another private collection.

Paper Filigree Cabinet

Filigree work – the decoration of furniture with coloured paper – gripped the attention of fashionable ladies for nearly two centuries. This flower-filled cabinet, made c.1780, is an ambitious and well-preserved example of the technique. "Mosaic work", as this painstaking art was often referred to in that century, involved rolling up tiny strips of coloured paper and sticking them to the surface of the piece to produce a decorative effect. In America filigree work was called quilling, because the paper was often rolled around a quill or feather.

Paper filigree developed as a less expensive form of gold and silver filigree, a technique that had been employed in the 15th century to decorate religious artefacts. During the 17th century this form of decoration became a popular hobby among well-to-do ladies blessed with the abundant free time it demanded. At its most complex the technique must have been extremely time-consuming, for some pieces contain as many as 135 rolls of paper per square inch, each applied separately.

Sets of the narrow paper strips, complete with patterns and instructions, were available to buy, and objects such as tea caddies, mirror frames, polescreens, and boxes were made to be embellished with the gaily coloured rolls of paper. Even royal ladies tried their hand at the absorbing pastime, among them George III's daughter Princess Elizabeth, who was given a box and a tea caddy to decorate.

The technique was also put to various other uses and often incorporated a wide range of materials. At the Lady Lever Gallery, Port Sunlight, where this cabinet is on display, there is a remarkable early 18th-century wax model of Queen Anne. The Queen's fashionable accessories, a flower-filled vase and the elaborate draperies in the background are largely made from paper filigree. Another cabinet in the same collection – at one time believed to be of Italian origin but now thought to be English (sadly, it is extremely faded) – is of particular interest because the filigree work, which depicts willow trees and pheasants, is partly made from rolled straw.

Above **Triangular rolls of paper attractively frame the print in the style of George Morland on the left side of the cabinet, while beneath, small birds are decoratively perched on sprays of verdant foliage.**

Right **The cabinet's simple shape and basic construction suggest that a provincial joiner made it for a lady to decorate.**

Such was the vogue for filigree work that patterns and an accompanying article appeared in the *New Ladies' Magazine*. The piece described the pleasure a lady might derive from the occupation: "The Art affords an amusement to the female mind capable of the most pleasing and extensive variety, it may be readily acquired at a very trifling expense."

This cabinet has been traced (by Lucy Wood of the Lady Lever Gallery) to William Angerstein of Wecting Hall, Norfolk, in 1895, and may have been made as a gift for his grandfather, John Julius, perhaps for or by one of his two wives. The piece is of rudimentary construction: the carcass is made from pine; and the fact that the backboard has been simply tacked in place suggests that it was made by a local joiner expressly for this type of decoration. By contrast with this simplicity, the filigree work is a *pièce de résistance* that few other surviving examples can rival. Almost every available surface, even the cornice and legs, is encrusted with the tight rolls of paper and then sprinkled with other decorative ingredients.

The filigree patterns themselves are created by varying both the colour of the paper and the way it is rolled. Flowers are created from lozenges of paper, leaves from small oval shapes, and a sunburst from triangular spokes. The lavishness of the overall effect is also contributed to by the contrast of the rolled paper with the textures of beads and pearls; and the addition of decorative prints and painted decoration. Oval-shaped coloured aquatints after George Morland depicting attractive ladies in pastoral settings have been pasted on to the centre of the doors and on each side, surrounded by a framework of pearl beads and "suspended" by a beaded *trompe-l'oeil* festoon.

151

When you open the doors a kaleidoscopic collage of colour and pattern assails you. The outer doors and the central inner cupboard are lined with satin that has been framed with coloured beads and carefully painted. A vase of flowers adorns one side, and a garland suspended by a ribbon the other, while on the inside of the central door is a botanical still life of a tulip with a butterfly and insect. The interior filigree work has been protected from damaging sunlight and remains vibrantly bright, much as it must have been when first complete. Flowers, leaves, arabesques, and garlands create a luxuriant field of colour and pattern over the various surfaces. The effect is one of such jewel-like brilliance that it is hard to believe that it was achieved with little more than paper.

Left **The outer doors and the inner central door are lined with painted silk floral decorations. The inner door conceals a compartment filled with filigree-faced drawers.**

Faux Bamboo Furniture

The combination of generous patronage and an imaginative designer given free rein resulted in these extraordinary pieces. Although they look as if they are made from bamboo, in fact they are beech carved and painted and complete with all the ridges, bumps, knots, and imperfections that you would expect to find in the real thing. "Faux bamboo" instantly conjured an exotic Eastern effect and therefore was ideally suited for use in the most dazzling of pseudo-oriental interiors: the Royal Pavilion at Brighton.

Above **This view of the Long Gallery, published in *Views of the Royal Pavilion, Brighton,* in 1826 by John Nash, shows the oriental interior designed by Frederick Crace.**

Once a modest farmhouse, the Royal Pavilion was acquired in 1787 by the Prince of Wales (later George IV), who transformed it into the most exotic of holiday homes. Rooms decorated in "Chinese style" had recently enjoyed a heyday but by this time the fashion had faded, and the decoration of the Royal Pavilion marked a resurgence of fascination with the arts of the East. Some of these pieces date from c.1802, when the Pavilion was given its first chinoiserie interiors. Others were made for the Long Gallery, where they now stand, and date from the second phase of decoration, which ended in 1823. The interior of the Long Gallery was masterminded by Frederick Crace, and much of the furniture he used was probably supplied by the leading furniture makers to the Prince: Elward, Marsh and Tatham.

Furnishing such an unconventional building demanded outlandish furniture, and so these pieces are a bizarre hybrid: European forms with an Oriental veneer. Regency furniture designers recognized two main ingredients in oriental furniture. If you combined lacquer with the ribbed stems of bamboo you encapsulated the flavour of the Orient. Bamboo permeated not just the furniture but almost every aspect of Crace's decorative scheme. The gallery was subdivided by narrow partitions of bamboo fretwork, and, most bizarrely of all, even the staircase was given the same Oriental treatment. Made from cast iron, it too was cast and painted to imitate bamboo.

The chairs contain a strange mix of chinoiserie and Gothic, with faux bamboo frame, caned seats, and a Gothic quatrefoil

Right **One of a pair of octagonal chinoiserie pedestals, made from bamboo and beech faux bamboo and decorated with japanned panels showing birds and flowers. Three pairs of pedestals were originally made, two of which pairs are now at Buckingham Palace.**

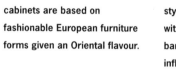

backrail. Others have odd lumps separating the weirdly shaped struts that make up the back splat. Most elaborate of all are the pedestals, two of which are original to the Pavilion and contain a mixture of faux bamboo, real bamboo, and japanned plaques in imitation lacquer. In Crace's final scheme the pedestals were shown flanking the chimney-piece and supporting Chinese export mandarin figures, and this is how they are seen today.

The faux bamboo cabinets that line the gallery continue the exotic theme: they are based on French Louis XVI commodes, but reinterpreted in whimsical oriental style. On some of them the brackets at the base are exotically moulded in fretted designs; grander versions have fretwork plinths (bases) designed as alternating arrowheads and concentric squares, and their tops are made from imitation marble held in place with elaborate fretted galleries. The central panels in the cabinet doors and sides were originally filled with panels of lustrous black and gold Japanese lacquer, but at some point the lacquer was removed and the panels in-filled with pleated red silk. The effect, while not to everyone's taste, is certainly extraordinary.

Left **The faux bamboo cabinets are based on fashionable European furniture forms given an Oriental flavour.**

Below **Elements of Oriental style are mingled improbably with Gothic motifs in this faux bamboo chair. The Gothic influence is seen in the pierced quatrefoil frieze that decorates the back of the piece.**

153

The Table of the Grand Commanders

Sober in subject yet sumptuous in treatment; modest in size yet monumental in the military supremacy it implies, this table is one of the most awe-inspiring legacies of Napoleon's patronage of the arts. Ironically, the table commissioned by the Emperor, and as ambitious in its own way as his military campaigns, ended up in the hands of his arch-rival George IV. The table was to become one of the English king's most treasured possessions and even featured in his coronation portrait, which showed George standing proudly beside it.

Right **Many leading artists were involved in the table's decoration, and the final cost of the piece was 29,025 francs. The heads and the imitation cameo scenes were painted by LB Parant, the low reliefs were by Antoine Béranger, and the bronze mounts were made by Pierre-Philippe Thomire.**

Above **In this portrait George IV stands beside the Table of the Grand Commanders.**

Right **The pivoted top can be turned and the *trompe-l'oeil* decoration viewed without the need to walk round the table.**

The top is made from a single huge plaque of Sèvres porcelain, painted with *trompe-l'oeil* cameos of the military commanders who gave the table its name. In the centre is Alexander the Great, surrounded by Hannibal, Julius Caesar, Pompey, and other outstanding leaders. So realistic are the cameos that it is hard to believe they are painted rather than carved from shell. Around them are painted scenes and architectural decorations in imitation low relief, all displaying great detail.

Napoleon likened his own empire to the military dynasties of the past, regarding himself as a latter-day Alexander the Great. To reinforce this association, he commissioned two matching tables from Sèvres, and this table's pair, turned down by King George IV and now at Malmaison, was painted with similar cameo portraits of Napoleon and his marshals. The paraphernalia of war dominated the "Empire style" that Napoleon nurtured as the artistic embodiment of his military prowess. The laurels, thunderbolts, lion masks, medallions, eagles, and stars that decorate this table all reflect his penchant for martial motifs. The central support, in the form of a bundle of arrows bound with an imitation leather strap, is derived from the Imperial Roman *fasces* – the insignia of a consul. (This motif decorated Marie Antoinette's jewel cabinet – *see* pages 44–5.)

The Sèvres porcelain factory, which had flourished under the patronage of the Bourbon kings Louis XV and XVI (*see* pages 130–1), fell into decline with the onset of the Revolution and production all but ceased. However, under Napoleon's rule

the factory enjoyed a new lease of life. Under the control of the state, and with a dynamic new director, Alexandre Brongniart, its production both improved and increased. As the name of Sèvres again became synonymous with porcelain of the highest quality, forms and designs changed to reflect the newly fashionable Empire style.

This complex and innovative work of art was commissioned in 1806 but not finished until 1812, cost nearly 30,000 francs, and demanded the skills of numerous artists, bronziers, gilders, and joiners. Among the technical problems it posed was how to support a huge sheet of hard paste porcelain on what is apparently a ceramic pillar. In the event a wooden carcass was used to support the top and this has a brass pivoting socket screwed to the underside into which slots a cylinder of metal, surrounded by the ceramic arrows, which in fact bear no weight at all. The pivot allows the table to be turned so that the viewer can admire the splendid *trompe l'oeil* decorations without having to walk around the piece.

The table's base is decorated with a motif of overlapping scales and sits on a curious crimson cushion. Remarkably, both base and cushion are ceramic and have no role but decoration. The table's stability comes from the metal plinth under the base, into which the metal core of the central pillar is fixed – a highly inventive solution to a major design problem.

Even as he waited to take possession of his extraordinary table, Napoleon's downfall was in prospect. As Prince Regent,

King George assembled an alliance of royal armies that joined forces against the Emperor and finally caused his abdication. By engineering the demise of Napoleon and the reinstatement of Louis XVIII, whom he had met while the French king was in exile in England, George had played a crucial role in maintaining the royal status quo in Europe. Ever a compulsive buyer of French art, George developed an almost obsessive desire to add to his collection items that had belonged to the defeated Emperor. He therefore sent his scouts to France to hunt out Napoleonic booty, and when he heard about the table he was especially eager to number it among his trophies. Learning of George's interest, the reinstated Louis made him a present of the piece, snatched from the jaws of "the exiled monster", as a sign of his profound gratitude. Much to George's excitement, the Table of the Commanders arrived at Carlton House, his London residence, in 1817. Three years later, on his accession to the throne, it was moved into the State Apartments at Buckingham Palace.

The King of Rome's Cradle

This spectacular silver-gilt cradle was made to celebrate the birth of Napoleon's son, the King of Rome. Presented to the Empress Marie-Louise by the city of Paris in 1811, the piece represents an outstandingly fruitful collaboration between three of France's most accomplished artists and craftsmen. Based on a design by the eminent French artist Pierre-Paul Prud'hon, the cradle was cast by the renowned goldsmith Jean-Baptiste Odiot, while the mounts were made by the leading worker in bronze of the day, Pierre-Philippe Thomire.

Above **The cradle in this portrait of the Empress Marie-Louise with her infant son is the second version based on Prud'hon's design and was intended for everyday use.**

The King of Rome was born on 20 March 1811, a year after his father's second marriage, to the eighteen-year-old daughter of the Austrian Emperor, Francis II. Napoleon's desire to establish a secure and enduring European empire made the provision of an heir crucial to his aims. After thirteen years of marriage Empress Josephine had failed to provide Napoleon with the children he craved, and consequently the marriage was annulled and Napoleon married Princess Marie-Louise.

Napoleon's tastes in furnishing and dress were relatively simple, but he was eager to boost French craftsmanship and industry. For this reason he was a keen patron of silversmiths, furniture makers, and porcelain manufacturers. Vast services of silver gilt were commissioned for use on state occasions and to celebrate the birth of his son.

The city of Paris was a similarly generous patron of Parisian silversmiths. Only a year before the King of Rome's cradle was made, it had presented Marie-Louise with a similarly lavish silver-gilt *toilette*, which included a table, a washstand, a ewer, an enormous cheval mirror, candelabra, a jewel box, an armchair, and a stool, to mark her marriage to Napoleon. After her husband's abdication this luxurious suite was taken by Marie-Louise to Parma, where she was installed as Duchess in 1815. At her instigation these priceless works of art were later melted down to provide funds to help the victims of cholera. The extraordinary cradle escaped a similar fate because it remained in Vienna, at the court of her father, the Emperor.

Above **A portrait of Napoleon's much-loved heir, the King of Rome. The unfortunate child was never to fulfil his proud father's expectations and inherit the empire: Napoleon was forced to abdicate three years after his birth. Exiled in Austria, the young man later died at the age of twenty-one.**

The baby's political significance is underlined by the expensive materials used for his cradle and by the decorations that cover it. The piece was not designed with practicality in mind, but as a means to assert royal power in much the same way as a ceremonial throne reinforces the status of a monarch. It originally stood on a raised dais, over which was suspended a ceremonial baldachin. A less extravagant cradle based on the same design was made for daily use and is now in the Musée Napoléon in the Château de Fontainebleau.

Prud'hon's design for the King of Rome's cradle highlights the lavishness of state furniture during the Empire period. The leading painter of Napoleon's court, he was admired by both Empress Josephine and Marie-Louise. He was drawing master to Marie-Louise, who is said to have been the model for his painting *Venus and Adonis*, now in the Wallace Collection.

The design of the cradle incorporates many of the motifs commonly found on important items of Empire furniture. The bees that link the grid-like side panels were a favourite Napoleonic symbol; the cornucopias that form the X-frame base are similar to those that adorn the Empress Josephine's bed at Malmaison (see pages 68–71); and the formally chased festoons of flowers are also typical of the period. The principal difference between this piece and other Imperial furnishings is that almost the whole cradle is constructed from silver gilt – a total of over 617lb (280kg) of silver was used.

The figurative elements of the cradle were all carefully chosen to reflect the royal occupant's importance. The base is supported by the figures of Justice and Power, while presiding over the niche in front of the celestial globe is the goddess of Glory, who carries a laurel wreath on which reposes a crown of stars, encircling the central star of Napoleon. Perched at the other end is an eagle, a symbol of both Imperial authority and the King of Rome. The cradle's sides are centred with two low-relief panels: one shows a figure representing the Seine, in whose arms Mercury places the newborn child; the other shows a personification of the Tiber contemplating the newborn star.

Sadly, despite the birth of a son, Napoleon was unable to maintain his grip on the empire he had fought so hard to create. Three years after his son's birth he was forced to abdicate and exiled to Elba. Meanwhile his beloved son was removed to the Austrian court and, despite Napoleon's pleas, prevented from visiting his father. In 1815 loyal Bonapartists proclaimed the boy Napoleon II, but five days later he was formally deposed. In 1818 the child was awarded the title of Duke of Reichstadt. He died in 1832 at the age of twenty-one and was buried in Vienna. A little over a century later, on the orders of Hitler, his body was reinterred in the Hôtel des Invalides in Paris. His priceless cradle had meanwhile remained part of the Austrian Imperial collection, and is now in Vienna's treasury, the Schatzkammer.

Below **Prud'hon's design for the King of Rome's cradle reflects both Napoleon's pride in his heir and the contemporary fascination with the classical world. The cradle features numerous motifs drawn from classical antiquity and was made from a luxurious combination of silver gilt and mother-of-pearl, lined in velvet and draped in silk and tulle, at a total cost of 152,289 francs.**

157

Regulator Clock
by A-L Breguet

A clock containing an oven seems an unlikely innovation, but at one time it was regarded as the ultimate in high-tech wizardry. The clock was made c.1820 by Abraham-Louis Breguet and his son, Antoine-Louis Breguet, the foremost clock makers in France in the early 19th century. One of the most unusual of the countless French objects that were acquired by King George IV for Carlton House, his residence in London, the clock is still in perfect working order and now stands in the Privy Purse Corridor at Buckingham Palace.

Above **This contemporary engraving shows Carlton House, the official residence of the Prince Regent (later George IV), which was reconstructed by Henry Holland at vast cost from 1783 to 1795, only to be demolished in 1826.**

Right **The regulator was positioned at the top of the Grand Staircase at Carlton House before being moved to Buckingham Palace, where it still remains.**

Like his father, George III, and others of his royal forebears, George IV was a passionate collector of clocks. But father and son had very different tastes, for while George III was fascinated by the technical aspects of horology, his son was far more interested in the look of a clock. French style appealed greatly to George IV's penchant for flamboyant furnishing (*see* pages 154–5) and accordingly, along with the top-quality pieces of Louis XVI and Empire furniture he bought, he also acquired numerous elaborate clocks from France's top makers. Nearly all the clocks George collected were visually spectacular; they included an amazing clock in the form of Apollo driving his chariot by Pierre-Philippe Thomire, a triple-dialled astronomical clock by Jean-Antoine Lépine, and a clock that depicted a sculptural tableau of The Oath of the Horath by Claude Galle.

This visually low-key regulator is very different from the ornate examples that George IV usually preferred and it is thought that it may have originally been designed not for him but for his enthusiastic, technically minded father. However, by the time the Breguets had turned their unusual idea into reality George III was suffering from advanced dementia. This was probably why they sent the detailed drawings, descriptions, and costings for the regulator to his son.

In the days before digital clocks, regulators were the most accurate timekeepers, providing large residences with a constant reliable record of time by which a visiting clock maker was able to regularly set all the other clocks in the house. Measuring

time in the most accurate way possible was the regulator's main job; its appearance was usually of secondary importance. The simple rectangular mahogany and glass case was a standard feature of regulators, although, as befits its royal owner, this is an elaborate example, with chased and gilded bronze mounts on the entablature and the base. Scientific exploration and invention were major preoccupations of that period and a movement of such refinement and complexity was in itself a great source of interest. This is one reason why the case has glazed panels on the front and sides. The glass also provided a more effective barrier than wood to changes in atmospheric conditions, while sealing the pendulums inside a glass case prevented variations in air pressure caused by their swing.

The clock is highly unusual in containing two separate movements, with two dials set side by side and two pendulums placed one behind the other. The main dial on the left shows the minutes of mean time; seconds and hours are shown on the subsidiary dials above and below. The right-hand dial shows the equation of time (the difference between solar and mean time) and the day of the month.

Each movement in the regulator is worked by a pin-wheel escapement driven by two large "gridiron" pendulums made from rods of alternating zinc and steel. The principle of the grid-iron pendulum was that the varying rates of expansion and contraction of different metals would ensure that the pendulum remained a constant length, and so no fluctuation would occur in its swing. Dual pendulums, reasoned the Breguets, were an advantage because pendulums positioned close to each other regulate and control each other, minimizing inaccuracy.

In the base of the clock there is a tiny, almost invisible hole. If you insert a small wire you can release the spring catch and a hinged front panel bursts open to reveal brass double doors enclosing a tray for burning charcoal – the unexpected oven in the clock. The stove is ventilated by a brass flue attached to the back of the case. The bizarre logic behind this device was that lighting the oven would help maintain a constant temperature and therefore assist perfect timekeeping. Fortunately, the oven was never used; if it had been, the heat could have caused irreparable damage to the clock.

The Breguets were so proud of their masterpiece that they exhibited it in 1819 at the Exposition des Produits de l'Industrie Française. In 1825 they eventually agreed to sell it to George IV for the considerable sum of £1000. In a letter to the king they described the clock as "a unique work, the most perfect and extraordinary that we have ever made". It was set up in Carlton House, at the top of the Grand Staircase, where doubtless a clock with an oven, as well as double pendulums, provided a talking point for George IV's distinguished visitors. Even those who knew nothing about clocks must have been surprised.

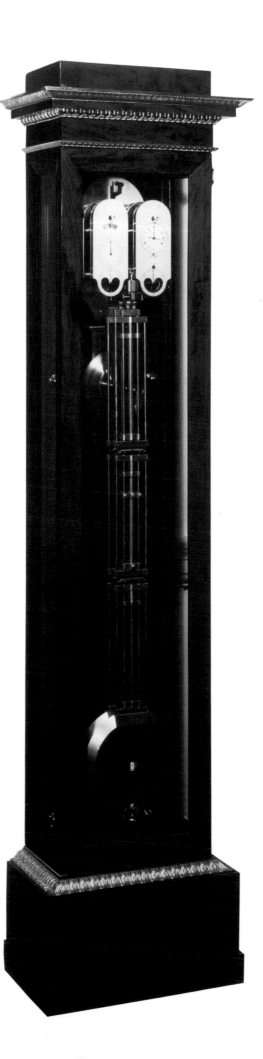

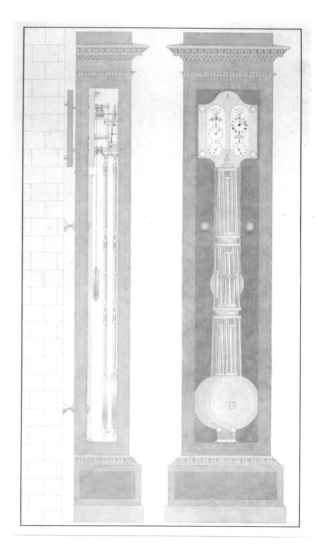

Left **The simple rectangular mahogany case and restrained gilt bronze mounts give the clock a rather modern appearance. The oven is hidden in the plinth and remains invisible unless a secret catch that controls a hinged panel is released.**

Above **In these detailed drawings sent by the Breguets to George IV, the diagram of the side shows the flue ventilating the concealed oven.**

159

Papier-mâché
Bedroom Suite

Mother-of-pearl, crushed pearl, gilding, and enamels have been combined here to create a bedroom suite that reveals Victorian taste at its most flamboyant. But what is most remarkable about this suite is the fact that it is made from papier mâché. This material became popular for furniture making in the 19th century, but because of the inherent fragility of papier-mâché furniture, very few large examples remain. The suite contains seven highly ornate pieces, including a bed, a wardrobe, a dressing-table, a mirror, and a towel horse, and is one of the finest collections of this unusual style of furniture to survive intact.

Above **The suite is on display at Lotherton Hall, near Leeds, in a bedroom whose furniture reflects the Victorian taste for innovative materials and flamboyant decoration.**

Below **A detail of the decoration on the wardrobe door shows how enamelling, gilding, and slivers of mother-of-pearl were applied to a japanned background to create the spectacularly rich effect.**

Although papier mâché has been made since ancient times, the seemingly impractical idea of constructing furniture from it became a reality only in the wake of the Industrial Revolution, when improvements in manufacturing techniques produced sheets of sufficient size and thickness. Papier mâché was made by gluing together ten or more layers of paper on a metal mould, soaking the result with linseed oil to seal it, and drying it. A patent for this process, whose finished product resembled plywood, was granted to Henry Clay of Birmingham in 1772. In 1847 the firm of Jennens & Bettridge, also of Birmingham, patented a process for applying steam to these papier-mâché panels, which allowed the substance to be moulded into an enormous variety of shapes. The material was usually finished by japanning and painting it in imitation of oriental lacquer (*see* pages 54-5), often with the addition of slivers of mother-of-pearl, gilding, and coloured decoration.

As its versatility and strength were exploited in new ways, papier mâché became the high-tech product of the age. British manufacturers based in the Birmingham area led the field in constructing furniture from papier mâché. Jennens & Bettridge, for example, became market leaders in the manufacture of papier-mâché items and may have been responsible for making this suite, although since none of the pieces is marked it is

impossible to be sure. The material was also used to make architectural decorations such as cornices and ceiling moulding that were less expensive than those carved from plaster.

However, while papier mâché also proved suitable for making trays, small boxes, buttons, and other small items, it was not generally robust enough to be used on its own in the manufacture of furniture. Probably the main reason why this bedroom suite has survived in such good condition is that much of the framework of the pieces is constructed from pine or metal and papier mâché was largely used just to fill in the spaces.

Papier-mâché furniture was among the exhibits displayed by British manufacturers at the Great Exhibition in London's Crystal Palace in 1851, where this suite is reputed to have been among the novelties. The bed is made from a combination of pine, cast iron, and papier mâché. The bed rails are metal, the spiral corner posts, legs, and feet are wooden, while papier-mâché panels form the head and foot. With characteristic Victorian exuberance, these panels were painted in brilliantly coloured enamels, to depict luxuriant bouquets, outlined with a hemisphere of crushed pearl shell, on a black lacquer ground.

The dressing-table and mirror are among the suite's most spectacular components. Their undulating shape shows how versatile papier mâché could be, and why the Victorians, with their insatiable appetite for ornament and elaboration, found the material so appealing. Extravagantly painted with sprays of roses, and clematis with trailing tendrils of gilt and a sprinkling of crushed shell, the dressing-table is crowned by an equally showy mirror with scrolled uprights supporting a curving frame on a three-drawer base. Here too the underlying structure is provided by pine, which has been used to make the frame and uprights, while the rest is papier mâché. But the most elaborate decoration of all is found on the doors of the wardrobe. Like a fertile indoor garden, this is a riotous tangle of bouquets of roses, lily of the valley, and clematis.

After its putative appearance at the Great Exhibition the suite is believed to have been used to furnish a private house in Birmingham (pages from a local newspaper were found lining the drawers). It had been removed to Cornwall by the 1930s, during which decade it was acquired for Lotherton Hall, near Leeds. Today the suite can be seen displayed there in an evocative 19th-century room setting.

Right **The mirror's scrolling supports and serpentine form reflect Victorian rococo revivalism. The drawers and the glass are framed by crushed shell, and the knobs and escutcheons are also shell.**

161

Antler Furniture

Hooves, horns, and antlers provided the inspiration for some of the most unusual 19th-century German furniture, which enjoyed a heyday in England in that century. The romance of Scotland, the Victorian appetite for baronial splendour, and the fascination with stags and deer, fuelled by Sir Edwin Landseer's memorable paintings and engravings, also played a part in the fashion for this naturalistic use of horn. These bizarre pieces were bought for Queen Victoria's Isle of Wight retreat, Osborne House, by her husband, Albert, the Prince Consort, perhaps to re-create the atmosphere of the German hunting lodges he had known in his youth.

Right **Horn furniture may have originated in hunting lodges, but this sofa, the largest example at Osborne, typifies the Victorian love of comfort. The horns are skilfully woven to provide the back framework and arms, and even the front rail is veneered in horn.**

Above **Osborne House, Isle of Wight, the home that Queen Victoria bought as a family retreat, describing it as "a place of one's own, quiet and retired". The house and gardens were designed by Prince Albert, who also chose many of the furnishings, including the horn furniture.**

Right **The Horn Room at Osborne was filled with examples of German horn furniture and remains much as it was when Prince Albert furnished it. After the Prince Consort's death little change was made to the interiors, and Queen Victoria died in the house in 1901.**

Horns have long been treasured as trophies of the hunt and from the earliest times they were mounted as mementoes of a feat of prowess. Since the Renaissance a chandelier adorned with horns had been a popular feature of German domestic interiors and it was a natural progression for craftsmen to use horn more boldly. By the early 19th century horn furniture, with a down-to-earth, "rustic" quality suitable for hunting lodges, began to be increasingly popular. The idea soon crossed the Channel and in 1803 Sheraton included a horn-legged chair in his *Cabinet Dictionary*, describing it as an ideal resting place "for one that is fatigued, as hunters generally are".

In 1851, when horn furniture was unveiled to the British public at the Great Exhibition in the Crystal Palace, London, German horn furniture began to be more widely sought after. One of the most notable early patrons was the Prince Consort, who anticipated the English demand when in 1844–6 he bought this selection of furniture for the Horn Room at Osborne House. Most of the pieces he selected were probably made by HFC Rampendahl, one of the leading manufacturers of such objects, who exhibited prominently at the Great Exhibition.

In America horns and antlers have long been regarded as emblems of the pioneering spirit that conquered the Wild West, and the 19th-century fashion for horn furniture outstripped

163

European demand and has endured throughout the present century. The astonishing versatility of horn, and the creativity of the 19th-century craftsmen who used it, is underlined by some of the contemporary advertisements, one of which mentions more than thirty horn products, ranging from sofas and chairs to thermometers and card cases.

The collection at Osborne includes a sofa, a footstool, six chairs, and a circular table. The intimate room in which they stand shows that the setting for horn furniture had by now metamorphosed from the rough and ready hunting lodge to the far more cosy environment of the parlour, where, surrounded by sporting paintings and portraits of favourite dogs, it formed an integral part of a typically cluttered Victorian interior.

Whether you find these pieces monstrously distasteful or intriguingly bizarre, there is no denying the inventive way in which the maker exploited the natural shape and texture of horn to create them. Horn is used for both structural and decorative elements in all the pieces, which take contemporary furniture as the starting-point for their design.

The centre table is veneered with pieces of horn inlaid with ivory stags and oak sprigs. Its top rests on a triple column of horn that is supported by a tripod base with ivory mounts and carved ivory paw feet. The serpentine-fronted sofa, with its plush button upholstery, also reflects standard patterns, but where a conventional sofa might have had a carved wooden framework and wooden feet, here the feet are made from six

stag hooves and the back framework is made from antler branches, punctuated with medallions of horn and ivory. The theme is continued in a matching foot stool, which also stands on four deer's feet and has a border (now rather dilapidated) made from horn tips and horn medallions.

Perhaps the most inventive use of horn is in the upright chairs, where nearly all the visible parts of the framework of the back and legs are made from stag's antlers, so that each chair in the set is slightly different. The jagged prongs of horn are woven together at the front, to save the chairs' users from becoming impaled, but at the back they stick out alarmingly. However evocatively "rustic" this might look, in such a crowded interior it must have been no easy matter to escape injury.

Crystal-glass Sideboard by F & C Osler

Above **A detail of the elaborate galleried frieze with which the base of the sideboard is decorated. The profuse cutting enhanced the refractive qualities of the glass.**

Right **Osler's design for the sideboard specifies each cutting pattern in minute detail. The pointed arches with scalloped edges reveal the fashion of the period for Islamic styles.**

The fragility of glass would seem to make it a highly unlikely material for use in the production of furniture. Nevertheless, during the 19th century the pioneering glass-makers F & C Osler made glass furniture of unprecedented scale and sophistication. Thrones, tables, settees, cradles, beds, and even bed steps were among the extraordinary range of glass furniture that the firm created, and this impressive sideboard, some 10ft (3.1m) in height, is rightly considered to be one of its most ambitious furnishing pieces.

Right **One of the largest and most impressive pieces of furniture ever made by Osler, the glass sideboard was almost certainly produced for the Far East, where such extravagant creations were a huge success.**

Combining furniture with glass was not a 19th-century idea. Glass had long been used to decorate expensive furniture: the jewel cabinet that Schwerdfeger made for Marie Antoinette (*see* pages 44–5) was richly decorated with *verre églomisé* panels, and similar decorative techniques were used in Baltimore in the early 19th century (*see* pages 66–7). However, throughout the 17th and 18th centuries glass was never more than a decorative element. Its use as a structural component was restricted by the problem of how to make pieces of glass of sufficient size, thickness, and strength to be suitable for use in furniture.

By the early 19th century, as improvements to industrial manufacturing processes enabled larger, thicker pieces of glass to be produced commercially, glass-makers in Russia, France, and England became increasingly adventurous. In the Imperial glass manufactory in Russia a handful of startlingly innovative pieces of glass furniture were made. In France the famous glass manufacturer Baccarat also produced a limited amount of glass furniture. But it was the English firm of Osler that, by the late 19th century, had established itself as the undisputed leader in the field.

The firm was founded in Birmingham in 1807 by Thomas Osler, who had previously trained as a surgeon but been unable to continue this profession after a riding accident. Although Osler's early years in business were not particularly successful, a change in fortune came when the company was taken over by his son Follett in 1831. A shrewd and ambitious businessman

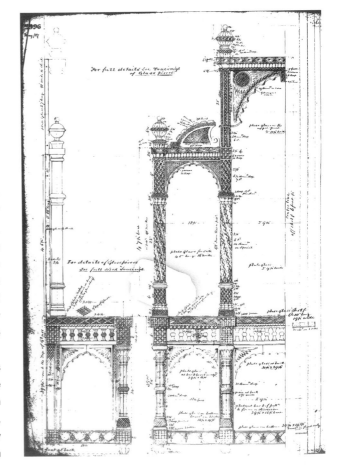

with great artistic flair, Follett lost no time in modernizing the manufacturing business by investing in new machinery. He also expanded the market for his goods by opening a showroom in London's Oxford Street.

The shop sold imported foreign glass as well as its own products and soon the firm's reputation as a leading glass dealer was such that it was enjoying the patronage of the Prince Consort, who bought a pair of candelabra for Queen Victoria, and Ibrahim Pasha, the ruler of Egypt, who commissioned the firm to make a pair of candelabra 16ft (4.9m) high to stand on each side of the tomb of the Prophet Muhammad at Mecca. But Osler's most famous piece was the massive crystal fountain that formed the appropriate centrepiece of Joseph Paxton's Crystal Palace at the Great Exhibition of 1851. This remarkable creation stood over 23ft (7m) high and made such a resonant noise that it had to be switched off while Queen Victoria gave her official opening speech.

Much of the company's financial success was due to expansion into the Far East, where it discovered a ready market for its increasingly fantastic furnishing creations. A showroom was opened in Calcutta, for by this time most of Osler's furniture was made for the Indian market, where wealthy clients had developed an apparently insatiable appetite for its opulent objects. Pieces such as this sideboard were invariably made by Osler without any particular buyer in mind, and then shipped to India to provide a spectacular talking point in the showroom, thereby attracting publicity and the attention of more and more moneyed customers.

But how did Osler manage to overcome the seemingly insurmountable technical problems involved in creating such a massive piece? The glass from which the sideboard is made is, in fact, a sparkling veneer applied to a wooden carcass. The load-bearing structural elements in the design, such as the columns that form the front of the base, are hollow tubes made of cut glass and containing a central core of metal. The outer surface of the metal is silvered and shiny like a mirror so that these sections create the illusion of being nothing but glittering crystal, with the metal inside virtually invisible.

In style the scalloped arches of the top and base reflect the mihrab (niche) of Islamic architecture. The powerful Islamic appearance of the overall design reflects widespread European interest, during the late 19th century, in the arts of the East, as well as the way in which Osler tailored designs to the taste of the Muslim princes who were among the firm's most prominent patrons. Every surface of the sideboard is suffused with an extraordinary range of patterns and designs. Crisply cut facets create surface texture, pattern, and myriad reflections with the intensity of diamonds. In the exotic setting of an Indian maharaja's palace the effect must have been literally dazzling.

165

Grotto
Furniture

Grotto furniture is by its nature sculptural and fantastic. It became popular in the 18th century and has remained so more or less to the present day. This style of furniture almost certainly originated in Venice, where the sculptural tradition had been firmly established for centuries. The suite shown here is ingeniously composed of the elements that decorate it: the arms of the chairs are fish, the legs are conch shells, the seats are formed from open scallops, and so on. This striking collection of pieces represents a fruitful marriage between nature and imagination.

Above **The grotto became a feature of many large English houses during the 17th century. This example was built at Woburn Abbey, Bedfordshire. Dating from c.1627, it is based on designs by the French garden architect Isaac de Caus.**

Right **One of the most imaginative pieces in the suite of grotto furniture seen here, this extremely realistic turtle is constructed from carved and painted wood. The shell is hinged and opens to provide a bizarre seat.**

Shells have a long history as a decorative motif. As symbols of natural beauty, they were prized by collectors, and they have featured almost without interruption in the art and architecture of antiquity and the Western world. Furniture has often used shells as decoration: fan-like scallops embellished baroque and rococo furniture, and the shell continued to be a favourite motif in the neoclassical period of the 18th century and beyond.

For centuries man's fascination with shells has gone hand in hand with a penchant for the curious, man-made caves known as grottoes, in which nature could be manipulated to create sites of exquisite beauty. By the end of the 18th century indoor and outdoor grottoes were as much a feature of the grand house as follies, fountains, and landscaped grounds, and the taste for grottoes continued into the next century. A haven for poetic or romantic contemplation, the grotto became a shrine to nature – but nature reinterpreted in fantastic form.

Furniture designed for the grotto was as impractical and imaginative as grottoes themselves. Chairs imitating gnarled tree roots and branches featured in Chippendale's pattern books, and similarly grotto furniture was made in Germany and elsewhere in continental Europe in the 18th century and later. In 19th-century Venice several workshops specialized in it, and this suite, unusual for the range and variety of pieces it contains, was made there by the leading firm of Pauly & Sons c.1880.

The naturalistic mother-of-pearl effect was produced by covering the carved wooden base with gesso (a mix of plaster of Paris and size) and then adding layers of silver leaf and coloured lacquer. Some of the pieces, such as the S-shaped confidante, are conventional 19th-century parlour furnishings reinvented in the form of shells. Others are more outlandish: the turtle on a rock pedestal is a seat. When you lift the turtle's head the shell swings back and the creature opens – not everyone's idea of a comfortable chair but certainly a novel one! Whimsical marine details are dotted throughout the suite. The turtle has a crab on its back that itself holds a shell. The writing table has an inkwell in the form of a scallop and a pen tray in the form of an enormous conch. The drawer fronts are modelled as shells, and if you pull on the central conch a writing slide appears.

There are some twenty-eight pieces in the group. How has this exceptionally large suite remained together and in such immaculate condition? It is believed to have been a honeymoon present, purchased in Venice in the late 1880s by a wealthy Englishman for his new bride. The couple are then thought to have settled in Australia. One can imagine that a grotto suite on this scale was not particularly appropriate in the outback of the turn of the century, and from 1905 it was stored in a warehouse in Sydney. There it remained, untouched and unused, until its recent rediscovery and appearance on the market.

Above **A pattern of settee widely used in comfortable 19th-century parlours was the S-shaped confidante. This imaginative example gives extravagant expression to the suite's marine theme with its conch-shell legs, scallop backrests, and arms inspired by mythical sea monsters.**

Right **Mussel shells, corals, and starfish adorn the table and mirror, while the chairs have scallop backs. But while it was imaginative, Venetian grotto furniture was not well made. The inner surface of the chair legs (visible on the chair on the left) is uncarved and its paint finish is crude.**

Carved Russian Chairs

Farming implements and furniture seem an unlikely mix, but among the extraordinarily diverse chairs made in Russia in the 19th century are some produced by makers who took rural equipment as their improbable theme and both constructed and decorated their creations with rustic artefacts. The other equally unconventional chair shown here is also probably Russian. It too is carved with powerful inventiveness, this time in the form of an eagle with impressive claws and fanned tail.

Right **A Russian balalaika provides an inventive back splat for the painted chair. Although the carving on this version is less detailed, the colourful painting adds to the chair's decorative appeal.**

Far Right **The origins of the eagle chair remain a mystery, but the eagle symbolizes power, suggesting that it was used by a figure of authority.**

Above **The *trompe-l'oeil* gloves at the back of the fruitwood chair are carved with great attention to detail, including an intricate geometric border and a realistic lining.**

Right **Traditional Russian folk art provides the inspiration behind the geometric patterns that decorate almost the entire surface of the chair. Even the axe blades are patterned.**

In Russian rural communities wood carving was a strongly established craft which developed from the necessity of making furniture and other objects for everyday use. Carving was used to embellish furniture, houses, and even agricultural implements such as the yoke used to harness a horse to a plough or cart. Furniture of this type was, of necessity, made from local wood. One of these chairs is made from fruitwood and elm, the other from painted birch or pine.

Both chairs were probably made by provincial craftsmen of considerable skill. Their structure and decoration combines expertly carved *trompe-l'oeil* objects and geometric pattern. Both have horseshoe-shaped main supports based on a yoke. In the centre the carved inscription in Cyrillic script reads, "Go gently and you go further". The arms of both chairs are carved highly realistically to resemble axes, with the blade of each embedded in a small log and the handle protruding through the yoke support. The back support on the painted version is carved in the form of a Russian balalaika. At the back of the seat of each chair, carved in realistic *trompe-l'oeil* manner, lies a large, well-worn glove, upturned and creased, as if just discarded by its owner.

The carved chair has a pierced seat, perhaps so that, on bitter winter evenings, a brazier could be placed beneath it to warm the occupant. Although it looks ungainly, the chair is very comfortable. The glove is positioned so that it does not get in the way when you sit down, and the seat is generously wide.

Almost the entire surface of both chairs is encrusted with traditional carved geometric designs, and the painted version additionally displays bright colours that reflect the lively patterns of folk art. Like all Russian furniture, chairs of this precise type are rare, but variants exist and there is a similar example in the Hermitage in St Petersburg.

No less unusual in its design, the eagle chair has arms formed from outstretched wings, while its feet provide the front legs and a fanned tail creates the rear support. The bizarre style in which the bird is portrayed, with tiny head, regimented feathers, and rather stiff, formal carving, suggests that it may have been made in Russia in the mid-19th century, although, as with so many inventive oddities, opinions differ. Chairs have always been used to denote status and the eagle has long been associated with military and political power. The powerful design, and particularly the high back, suggests that the chair may have been the seat of an official or a person of authority.

While the bird is carved in a manner that places it outside European traditions, a precedent exists in a vase from the Treasury of Saint-Denis, now in the Louvre in Paris. Mounted with a 12th-century silver eagle's head, wings, and legs, it echoes the style of this chair, whose design was perhaps inspired by the 19th-century fascination with medieval times.

171

Dressing Table and Chairs by Antoni Gaudí

A gravity-defying dressing table with weirdly distorted legs and a mirror that seems uncomfortably askew; seats that look as if they have been made from melted wood or carved bones. It is little wonder that Antoni Gaudí has frequently been accused of being "untempered by considerations of tradition or good taste". Nevertheless, the originality of his approach to furniture remains unquestionable, and these pieces, from two of his major architectural commissions, the Güell Palace and the Casa Calvet, both in his adopted city of Barcelona, are outstanding examples of the architect and designer's uniquely eccentric imagination.

Right **Simple in construction but complex in design, the various forms of seating that Gaudi designed for the Casa Calvet in Barcelona illustrate his enduring preoccupation with the human form.**

Above **Recalling the entrance to a Gothic castle, the main vestibule of the Güell Palace is adorned with huge cast-iron gates that are decorated with imaginative scrolled motifs. Their strange, elongated horseshoe shape reflects a synthesis of Gothic and Arabic architectural styles.**

Right **The roof of the Güell Palace is as inventively decorated as the gates, with its chimneys and ventilation outlet in weird turreted shapes and encrusted with a variety of ceramic tiles and stones.**

The son of a coppersmith, Gaudí was born in Reus, on the Catalan coast, in 1852. Although as a child he was dogged by ill health, he developed a keen interest in his surroundings, and at seventeen began studying architecture in Barcelona. As an architect Gaudí designed his outlandish furniture to fit in with his equally extraordinary buildings. Whether it was a house, a palace, or an office, his schemes were unified to the extent that the structure of a building was woven into the very fabric of its decoration, which in turned fused with the interior. So much so in fact that in many cases it is difficult to tell where building ended and furniture began.

Gaudí's designs may be regarded as the most extreme manifestation of the Catalan style, a bizarre sculptural offshoot of the Art Nouveau movement that flourished in other European centres at the end of the 19th century. Unlike most of Spain at this time, Barcelona experienced a period of great economic prosperity. Its population had quadrupled during the latter half of the 19th century and industries such as iron and cotton had created a prosperous society, a number of whose wealthier members were increasingly prepared to patronize artists and craftsmen. Gaudí found as his clients several *nouveau riche* businessmen who were enthusiastic about his branching out from conventional styles of architecture or furniture.

Built for his friend Eusebi Güell between 1866 and 1889, the Güell Palace was one of Gaudí's first major commissions. Güell, a self-made brick manufacturer with a keen interest in the arts and social reforms that he had encountered in England, made his home a haven for young artists and he and Gaudí became firm friends. The exterior of the house is relatively small and unspectacular, although the fantastically decorated roof, studded with an assortment of mushroom-like turrets, foretells what lies within. The interior conjures up baronial splendour, with its grand hall spanning three floors crowned by a cupola. Elsewhere in the house heavily ornamented wooden ceilings continue the extravagance, and the furniture is outrageously baroque in its complexity and lavishness.

The dressing table reflects the influence of Art Nouveau design in its sculptural appearance and combines a variety of materials – wood, metal, glass, and gilding – to produce an unusually decorative effect. The design includes a strange, pod-shaped integral stool on the right-hand side and the three legs on this side are curiously ribbed to give the impression of twisting tendons and sinews. On the other side the legs are of a completely different design: stiff and formal with strangely eccentric bumps shaping their inner profile. The table's top is formed as if moulded from dough rather than carved from wood, and has a curved frieze that terminates in thick ripples. Similarly, the frame surrounding the mirror looks as if it is made from a ribbon and ends in ruffled heaps that spill luxuriantly on

to the strange, barrel-like compartments on either side. The wood's surface is etched with carved ripples and flower-like motifs that were once richly gilded and in the centre a sweeping metal strut gives support to the strange, lop-sided creation.

Less opulent but no less extraordinary are the chairs made for the Casa Calvet in 1898–1900. Gaudí designed this house, in an elegant residential quarter of Barcelona, for Pedro Martín Calvet, an industrialist. Compared with earlier designs, it was relatively restrained, and its less sumptuous furniture reflects his move towards more streamlined, less cluttered forms.

Flat sections such as the backrests and seats are formed from blocks of wood joined around a central plank with the grain running concentrically. The seats are made from solid oak and

are of simple, almost rustic construction. They are, however, shaped and carved in a completely unconventional manner. Swellings, dips, and undulations feature on the front and back of seat and backrest and their surfaces are carved and pierced with naturalistic floral decorations. The shape of the upturned arms, the strange ribbed supports that hold the backrest and the legs, and even the profile of the backrest make one think of bones or natural organic forms. Despite the chairs' apparent eccentricity and freedom from the constraints of tradition, the design is more carefully calculated than it might appear. The arm rests and sculpted seat are carefully moulded to match the shape of the human body. This was a recurring theme in much of Gaudí's furniture; indeed, while designing a park bench, he is said to have asked a workman, in the interests of ergonomics, to take off his clothes and sit on the plaster version.

With the benefit of hindsight, Gaudí's unique achievement is nowadays increasingly appreciated. The rather austere house in which he once lived is now home to the Museo Gaudí, where the furniture shown on these pages, along with many other extraordinary pieces, stands as a powerful reminder of his liberated approach to design.

Left **With its lop-sided mirror and contorted asymmetrical legs, the dressing table designed for the Güell Palace must rank as one of Gaudí's most bizarre creations.**

Below **Like many of Gaudí's furniture designs, this carved oak chair designed for the Casa Calvet reflects, in its strange organic form, the influence of Art Nouveau.**

Right **Gaudí designed his furniture to suit his interiors. The heavily carved table and chairs in the Güell Palace's dining room harmonize with the panelled walls and the elaborate chimneypiece.**

174

Cabinets and Chairs
by Carlo Bugatti

Carlo Bugatti's unmistakable furniture is exotic, eclectic, and above all highly original, displaying the renowned Italian designer's passion for unfamiliar materials, highly unusual decoration, and outlandish form. The cabinet, display stand, and chair shown here weave together strands borrowed from Japanese art, Arabic calligraphy, Moorish architecture, and tribal artefacts, mixing wood with various metals, bone, parchment, and silk, to produce bizarre objects that flout the conventions of both Western and Eastern art.

Above **A bedroom created c.1900 by Bugatti for Lord Battersea's London residence reveals the designer's taste for bizarre, orientally inspired decorative schemes.**

Right **This striking cabinet, made around the turn of the century, features a central panel that resembles a giant keyhole, centred with a large silk-fringed tassel, and inlays of bone and coloured metal.**

The father of the world-famous car designers and engineers Ettore and Jean Bugatti, and grandfather of the renowned sculptor Rembrandt Bugatti, Carlo Bugatti was a native of Milan. After training at the Milan School of Art and the École des Beaux-Arts in Paris he began designing furniture towards the end of the 19th century, and immediately developed a fiercely individualistic style. Like Antoni Gaudí, his equally idiosyncratic counterpart in Spain (*see* pages 172–5), Bugatti usually designed furniture as part of a complete room, and seen *en masse* his strange objects created unreal, almost dreamlike settings. His rise to public prominence was accelerated after the 1902 Turin International Exhibition, where four rooms that he designed attracted enormous attention.

Imaginative design was combined with unusual materials to create a very unconventional repertoire. The furniture was loaded with trademark vellum or parchment, fringing, bone, and metal inlays. Colours were strangely subdued, even painted decoration was nearly monochromatic, and additional visual interest was supplied chiefly by the contrasting textures of the varied ingredients and by intricate and extensive decoration.

In using such strange materials Bugatti was obliged to overcome various practical problems. He developed a glue that allowed parchment to adhere to wood. Strips of beaten copper, brass, and pewter provided elaborate decorative inlays, and the skill with which this was achieved was often superior to the craftsmanship of the North African artefacts on which he drew.

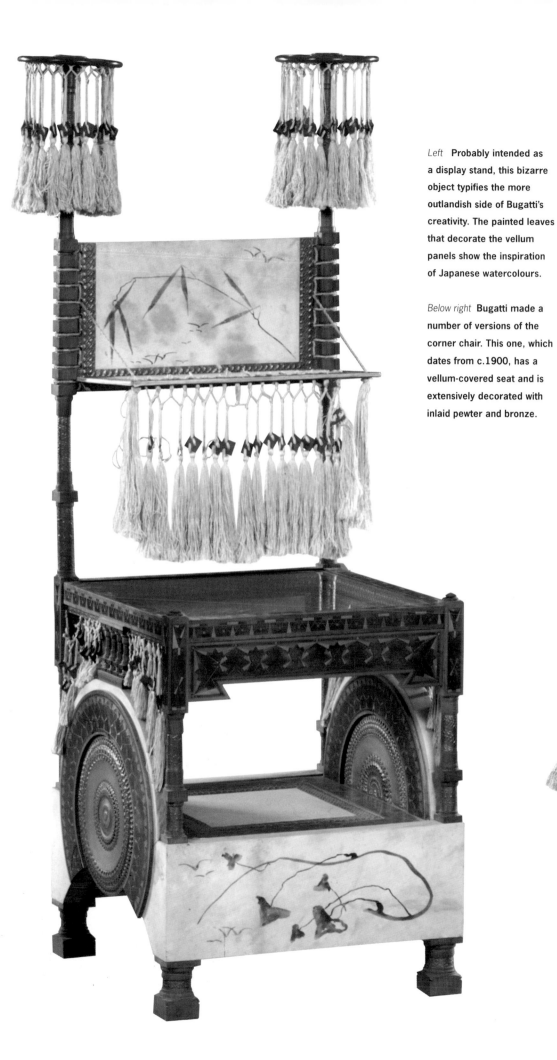

Left **Probably intended as a display stand, this bizarre object typifies the more outlandish side of Bugatti's creativity. The painted leaves that decorate the vellum panels show the inspiration of Japanese watercolours.**

Below right **Bugatti made a number of versions of the corner chair. This one, which dates from c.1900, has a vellum-covered seat and is extensively decorated with inlaid pewter and bronze.**

The display cabinet shown here is an example of the way in which Bugatti reinvented conventional furniture forms. Like many of his masterpieces, this remarkable object begs the question, "What is it?" It looks like a chair, but since it has a shelf suspended from the backrest, and a drawer in the centre beneath a glazed top and base, it was probably intended to be a display stand. Perhaps the strange, saucer-like discs hung with tasselled fringes that flank the back are also meant to be used for displaying suitably exotic works of art. In typical Bugatti fashion the stand combines elements derived from a variety of international artistic traditions. The back and base are covered in vellum painted in a manner reminiscent of Japanese watercolours, and the sides, inlaid with panels of pewter and brass, recall Moorish architecture.

A similarly odd selection of motifs are mingled in the corner cabinet. Here the shelf and door panel are covered in vellum and the decoration is made from a combination of wrought copper and bone, and coloured metal inlay. In overall form this is a less cluttered, more architectural piece, and the pointed arches that form the upper part are clear references to the mihrab of Islamic architecture. Although in theory all the pieces shown here could be used, Bugatti's furniture is not primarily intended to be practical. These were objects whose appeal lay in their irreverence, their lack of convention, and, above all, their inventiveness. For this designer, durability and practicality were not part of the equation.

177

Trompe-l'oeil Furniture by Wendell Castle

The tenuous dividing line between furniture and sculpture is explored by these pieces of trompe-l'oeil furniture made by Wendell Castle, one of America's leading woodworking craftsmen. Castle creates visual puns with ordinary pieces of furniture by fusing them with illusionistic sculpture of equally routine objects. A carved trench coat has attached itself to a coat rack; a briefcase and a pair of gloves are carved on to the surface of an elegant Chippendale side table; and even an upholstered chair seat is realized in wood.

Above **Wendell Castle has returned several times to the theme of the traditional side table on which contemporary objects are depicted in carved form. Other versions feature tables of various styles and such objects as tablecloths, keys, and a scarf.**

In his *trompe-l'oeil* furniture Castle adopts a tongue-in-cheek approach to the question of where sculpture begins and furniture making ends, and as a result these pieces are entertaining as well as functional. Essential to the illusion he creates is his skilful manipulation of wood to represent a variety of materials and textures. The squashy felt hat, the well-worn briefcase, and the classical brass handles and escutcheons are all depicted, with unerring fidelity, in wood. *Coatrack with Trench Coat*, made in 1978 from Honduras mahogany, is carved to portray exquisite detail – even the buttonhole and button are clearly defined – and convince us that wood has metamorphosed into floppy cloth. And yet, despite its whimsical decoration, the rack could still function as somewhere to hang your coat – if it was not on display in the Houston Museum of Fine Art.

Born in 1932 in Kansas, Castle has, since the 1960s, established himself as one of the pioneers of America's renewed interest in the use of natural materials for making hand-crafted furniture. He decided at an early age that he would become a designer in one field or another, and after studying design at Kansas University he decided to concentrate on sculpture. But by 1961, when he moved to New York, he had begun to produce furniture, realizing that objects made from wood could synthesize and transcend both disciplines.

Castle's earliest work revealed his reaction to the machine-manufactured furniture of the 1940s and 1950s. Capitalizing on the ideology of the 1960s, he fused organic shapes with natural

Right **The coatrack in this piece is made using the stack laminated technique. Castle developed this method in the 1960s to allow him to make the biomorphic furniture that characterized his early career.**

materials and used emphatically hand-crafted techniques that machines could not rival. Early trademark pieces – for example, an undulating cherrywood two-seater sofa that is now in the Metropolitan Museum of Art, New York, and an apple-wood blanket chest in the University of Rochester Art Gallery – reveal Castle's strong reaffirmation of the role of craftsman – an idea that was pioneered in England in the work of John Makepeace. Castle explained the reasons behind his interest in sculptural wooden furniture in this way: "My quest as an artist has been primarily involved with the imaginative transformation of organic form – a quest which was first seriously undertaken in the art nouveau period. I'm also interested in giving a piece of furniture a personality, a presence." Like Makepeace, Castle went on to disseminate his approach to furniture making by establishing a school – the Wendell Castle Workshop in Scottsville, outside Rochester, New York State.

For his early pieces Castle employed very simple furniture-making techniques because he had received no formal training in this field. His distinctive sculptural style attracted instant attention, and he has continued to receive wide acclaim both for his unconventional abstract furniture and for more traditionally inspired objects such as these.

Stacked laminated wood, Castle's most characteristic technique, was used for *Coatrack with Trench Coat*. In this method, which he developed early in his career, he glues together strips of wood in a large block that roughly follows the final form, and then carves this to create the finished object. In contrast, in the maple *Chair Hung with Sports Coat*, likewise made in 1978, and the mahogany and zebra wood *Side Table with Hat and Brief Case*, also from 1978, Castle uses traditional furniture-making techniques and long-established furniture styles and only the sculpted object is made from laminated wood. Chair and table reflect the classical forms of American Chippendale and Sheraton-style furniture, yet by linking them to modern everyday objects such as a sports coat and a briefcase he gives them a contemporary relevance.

Where did Castle get the idea for his illusionistic furniture? In 1976, while teaching sculpture students at New York's Brockport University to draw a coat hanging on a chair, he was struck by the challenge of translating such ordinary objects into wooden sculpture. Clearly such an idea would not work unless the sculpture was extremely realistic. Castle employed a French carver to teach him to create convincing *trompe-l'oeil* objects, and by 1978 he was producing works like those seen here.

Are they sculpture or furniture? Where does craftsmanship end and art begin? Perhaps such questions are irrelevant, for what really matters is the blend of imagination and technical know-how that enabled these exceptional pieces to be made and to be enjoyed as you choose.

Below **Castle's capacity for minute observation allows him to display virtuoso carving in his striking *trompe-l'oeil* furniture. Note the tiny pleat in the "fabric" forming the corner of the chair seat.**

179

Yacht Fittings and Furniture

This collection of furniture merits inclusion for its extraordinary location – on board one of the world's largest privately owned yachts. Around 371ft (113m) in length, this elegant vessel has six decks and an extensive crew. When she first made contact her owner wanted us to make one piece of furniture. However, as our rapport blossomed through an exceptional relationship of understanding, so the commission grew. As a result, the furniture that we designed for the yacht turned into one of our most important commissions ever.

Above **The lid of a small box that we presented to the owner of the yacht when the commission was successfully completed was appropriately decorated with a marquetry picture of the vessel.**

Naturally, we had to bear in mind the maritime environment in designing these pieces. Sea air is not kind to furniture, and so delicate woods and veneers had to be well protected by a more resilient finish than would otherwise have been used. Stability in high seas was another important consideration, so all the large pieces were made with bases that could be bolted to the floor.

The sea provided us with a richly varied decorative theme for much of the furniture we supplied, and two motifs that recur in many of the pieces are shells and "C" scrolls. The furniture we were commissioned to make included a bar, a variety of tables, chairs, cabinets, writing desks, mirrors, bed panels, and ottoman stools. As with any piece of furniture, the colour of the wood and the design of each piece helped to set the style for each room. Pale woods and simple, uncluttered shapes are keynotes of the furniture made for informal areas of the yacht; while pieces made for the more formal rooms employ richly coloured veneers such as rosewood and ebony, lavish gilding, and more complex designs, all of which elements combine to create an ambience of distinctive splendour.

The huge bar, made for an informal seating and dining area, was the single largest piece we created. Spacious, light, and airy, this part of the vessel has pale sycamore floors. The piece of furniture clearly had to harmonize with this setting, perform a function, and provide a focal point. Its design is distinctive, both for its size – the top is 13ft (4m) long and 4ft (1.2m) wide – and for the intricate marquetry with which it was decorated.

Left **Small sycamore side tables made to stand on each side of a sofa in the informal seating area were decorated with a blend of marquetry and applied decoration. The "C" scroll border on the top reflects the border of the carpet (visible right).**

Right **These solid-sycamore dining chairs, upholstered in fine white leather, were intended to harmonize with the existing circular marble-topped dining table and with the pale sycamore floors.**

In the frieze that surrounds the base of the bar a wealth of elaborate marine detail is painstakingly depicted in marquetry: scallops and starfish intertwine with corals, conches, cones, and rippling seaweed. The boarded floor of the beach-bar area was also reflected in the sides of the bar by the use of alternating panels of ripple and straight-grained sycamore. This arrangement produces a striped effect that brings alive these large, flat areas.

Elsewhere the shell motif was used not only in the form of inlaid marquetry design, but also as applied decoration. Among the other pieces we designed for this room were small side tables made from solid sycamore with ripple sycamore inlays. Their circular tops had a band of inlaid "C" scrolls cut from inlay

of dyed sycamore and the frieze supporting the top and the plinth base were studded with carved ebonized shells. The same wood was also used at the base of the column supports and as a moulding on the plinth.

One of our simplest but, as it turned out, most effective designs was a set of upholstered dining chairs. The frames are made from solid sycamore, inlaid with richly coloured rosewood, ebony, and satinwood. The chairs' crisp, clean-cut form seems ideally suited to the marine setting and the design has proved so successful (there are now more than forty on board) and so comfortable that we asked the owner for permission to use the same design for chairs to sell in our shop, where they have also proved popular.

Forming a marked contrast with the light woods that we selected for the furniture in this area were the richly figured pieces we produced for the more formal areas of the yacht. The vessel contained a substantial collection of works of art in Art Deco style, among which was a boldly patterned carpet based on a design by Ruhlmann. The carpet had been commissioned from a New York manufacturer for use in the formal reception area. Taking its jagged geometrical pattern as our theme, we furnished the wall of this area with a large mirror and decorated its frame with marquetry of the same powerful design. In the yacht's formal saloon, among the various tables that we designed were a striking pair of console tables. Opulently veneered with rosewood, these pieces were supported by fluted columns made from satinwood and ebonized sycamore and enriched with gilded detail.

In many other parts of the yacht we continued the maritime theme. Some of the most intricate marquetry is to be found on two panels on either side of a narrow corridor. Each of these highly decorative designs was based on astrological insignia and the subjects we chose were, appropriately, the water signs of Pisces and Aquarius.

For our design team, this was a particularly challenging and exciting project. The whole commission, masterminded by a single member of the team, took six months to complete and called on the skills of numerous craftsmen. All those involved recall with pleasure the remarkable relationship we built up with our patron. Her active participation in the development of the project inspired each design and ensured that the furniture we made both stimulated and reflected her taste. The harmonious interiors of her yacht are a testimony to the significance of the patron's influence – and, we reflect with great pride, on the role that we played in helping her to achieve her aims.

182

Above **Panels representing the astrological water signs of Pisces (seen here) and Aquarius were made from a combination of nine woods, including ripple sycamore, burr ash, grey and blue sycamore, maple, box, and Swiss pear.**

Right **The marine motifs used to create the frieze on the base of the bar are continued on the top. Each corner is inlaid with a scallop shell cut from light- and dark-grey sycamore, and shells likewise decorate a central panel.**

Above **The marine life that inspired much of the yacht's furniture is represented in the marquetry used to decorate the base of the enormous bar. The design incorporates coral, shells, and starfish, all of which were created from an intricate assortment of woods.**

Glossary

Acanthus Stylized, leaf-shaped ornamentation representing the plant *Acanthus spinosus*, popular in classical architecture and often used as a carved motif on furniture.

Amphora Classical two-handled vase used for storage. Vases of this shape were popular decorative motifs on neoclassical furniture.

Anthemion Decorative flower motif representing the honeysuckle. Derived from ancient Greek art, it was widely used on furniture in the neoclassical period.

Applied decoration Decoration, usually carved or moulded, made for application to a piece of furniture.

Apron Band or shaped skirt of wood that fills in the space between the legs and is attached to the top of a table or chest of drawers, or runs beneath the seat rail of a chair.

Arabesque Decoration made from elaborate, intertwined leaves and scrolls.

Arcading Series of decorative linked arches derived from architecture.

Backboard Unfinished plank of wood used, with others, to form the back of most case furniture intended to stand against a wall.

Baluster Slender, elongated, vase-shaped pillar with a bulbous base – a common form for legs and pillars.

Banding Veneer cut into narrow strips and applied to create a decorative effect; usually found around the edge of tables or drawer fronts.

Barley twist Spiralling columns – a popular form for legs and chair backs in the 17th century.

Block front Distinctive form of construction that usually consists of two convex vertical sections flanking one concave central section. A style particularly associated with furniture made in the Newport, Rhode Island, area in the 18th century.

Bombé Term used to describe furniture that has a swollen, outward-curving form, associated with 18th-century continental case furniture.

Bonheur du jour Small, versatile ladies' writing desk that became popular in France and England in the 18th century.

Boulle marquetry Decorative inlay named after André-Charles Boulle, using tortoiseshell and various other materials, such as brass, pewter, ivory, and mother-of-pearl. Developed in the late 17th century, the technique remained popular until the 19th century.

Bow front Furniture with an outward-curving front – a popular form for sideboards and case furniture from the late 18th century onwards.

Bracket foot Foot of squared form, sometimes with a shaped inner profile, commonly found on 18th-century furniture.

Breakfront Term used to describe a piece of furniture with a prominent central section, usually seen on sideboards and bookcases of the 18th century.

Broken pediment Central opening in the line of a pediment, typically filled with an urn or a sculpture.

Bun foot Foot of rounded and sometimes rather squat form, typical of case furniture of the William and Mary period (c.1690–1700).

Burr Veneers cut from the base or other parts of a tree where the wood is tightly figured.

Cabriole leg Leg of elongated and gently curving "S" shape, popular in Europe from the late 17th century onwards.

Carcass Main structure of a piece of furniture, to which veneers are applied.

Cartouche Carved decoration that imitates an unfurled paper or parchment scroll.

Caryatid Sculpted female figure used as a pillar to support an entablature, as in classical architecture.

Case furniture Furniture designed primarily for storage, such as chests of drawers, bureaux, cupboards, and cabinets.

Cassone Italian chest, often part of a dowry, elaborately decorated with painting and carving, and often made in pairs.

Chest-on-chest Tall chest of drawers, mounted on another similar, slightly larger chest, and usually in two sections. Also known as a tallboy.

Chevron Linked zigzag motif popular in carved form in medieval furniture and revived in the 19th and 20th centuries.

Chinoiserie Western decoration in pseudo-oriental style.

Commode Elaborate French form of chest of drawers, often highly decorated and extremely popular throughout Europe in the 18th century. The term was also used by the Victorians to denote a chamber-pot chair or cupboard.

Console table Side table with two front legs, supported at the back with brackets attached to the wall (*see also* Pier table).

Cornice Projecting moulding forming the top part of an entablature.

Cornucopia Decorative motif in the form of a goat's horn full of flowers and fruit, and symbolizing fertility and plenty.

Cresting Carved decoration surmounting a piece of furniture.

Cross-banding Veneered edge where the grain runs at right angles to that of the main wood.

Dentils Small, teeth-like, rectangular block projections derived from classical architecture and often used as part of a frieze on furniture.

Dovetail Joint formed by small, wedge-shaped, interlocking tenons.

Ébéniste French furniture maker who specialized in making veneered furniture such as desks, cabinets, and commodes (as opposed to a *menuisier*, who made carved furniture).

Ebonize   To paint, stain, or lacquer wood to imitate ebony.

Escutcheon   Metal embellishment around a keyhole, often of brass, and sometimes elaborately shaped and covered with a hinged plate.

Feather banding   Decorative effect achieved by laying strips of veneer in opposite diagonals to each other. Also known as herringbone banding.

Festoon   Decorative motif in the form of a suspended garland of flowers.

Fielded panel   Part of a door or other flat area separated from a surrounding frame by angled or bevelled edges.

Figuring   Pattern created by the grain of the wood.

Finial   Decorative motif that most often protrudes from the top of a piece of furniture.

Fluting   Series of decorative semicircular grooves derived from classical architecture and usually incised in the surface of a column or leg.

Fretwork   Carved border made from interlocking straight lines – a popular form of decoration in Chinoiserie furniture.

Gesso   Plaster-like substance, from size, whiting, and linseed oil, used to prepare wood for gilding, japanning, and painting.

Gilding   Decoration achieved by applying gold leaf or gold dust to the surface of a piece of furniture.

Highboy   American term for a chest on a stand.

Inlay   Method of decorating furniture by insetting small pieces of wood or other materials into carved-out areas of a solid piece of furniture (as opposed to marquetry, which uses veneers).

Japanning   Pseudo-oriental lacquer made in the West.

Klismos   Chair with outward-curving sabre legs of classical Greek origin.

Lacquer   Type of highly polished varnish made from gum extracted from the Far Eastern tree *Rhus vernicifera* and used to decorate screens and other objects.

Lowboy   Small side table with drawers and usually with short cabriole legs.

Marquetry   Decoration produced by using veneers of different woods to create a design or picture.

Oyster veneering   Decorative effect made by using veneers cut at right angles to the grain of the branch (resembling the patterns of an oyster shell). Olivewood, walnut, and laburnum were popular woods for this technique.

Papier mâché   Material made from pulped paper and moulded into various forms before being dried; popular for furniture making in the 19th century.

Palmette   Decoration in the form of a fan, derived from a palm leaf.

Parquetry   Geometric marquetry design made from veneers of various woods.

Patera   Decoration in the shape of an oval or circular medallion.

Patina   Accumulation of polish and dirt that enriches and softens the colour of furniture as it ages.

Pier table   Small side table made to stand against a wall between two windows.

Pietre dure   Decorative technique using inlays of semi-precious stones – a speciality of Florentine craftsmen from the 17th to the 19th century.

Pilaster   Flat decorative pillar derived from classical architecture.

Relief   Decoration that is moulded or carved and raised from the surface.

Roll-top desk   Popular form of writing desk in the 18th century, with a curved lid that slides upwards and is housed in the carcass when the piece is opened.

Sabre leg   Outward-curving leg, shaped like the curved blade of a sabre, that became fashionable on late-18th-century Empire and Regency-style chairs.

Secretaire   Form of writing furniture with a flat front that drops down to provide a writing surface and conceals a range of compartments and pigeon-holes.

Splat   Central piece of wood in the back of a chair that connects seat and top rail; it can be decorated in many ways.

Stretcher   Rail joining legs on chairs, tables, and other forms of furniture to provide additional strength.

Stringing   Fine lines of wood inlaid into the surface of the main wood to produce contrast.

Tallboy   *See* Chest-on-chest.

Tester   Wooden or fabric canopy used to cover a bed.

Trompe l'oeil   Illusionistic decoration intended to look so realistic as to "deceive the eye".

Turning   Craft of shaping wood on a lathe to create even, circular forms and patterns, developed as an economical way of using expensive woods and for highlighting decorative grain.

Veneer   Thin strips of wood used to cover and decorate the surface of a piece of furniture.

Verre églomisé   Glass decorated on the reverse with painted decoration and backed with metallic foil. Popular in ancient times, the technique was revived in 18th-century France and named after one of its chief exponents, Jean-Baptiste Glomy.

Vitruvian scroll   Decoration formed from a series of interconnected, wave-like "C" scrolls, named after the famous Roman architect Vitruvius.

Volute   Spiralling scroll used to decorate the capital of an Ionic column.

185

Where to visit

The following listing includes only those objects featured in this book that are on public display.

AUSTRIA

Cylindrical Secretaire, *p52*:
MAK, Stubenring 5,
Vienna

The King of Rome's Cradle, *p156*:
Museum Kunsthistorisches,
Vienna, Austria

CZECHOSLOVAKIA

Metamorphic Library Steps, *p120*:
Museum of Czechoslovak
Literature, Prague

FRANCE

The Bureau du Roi, *p38*:
Château de Versailles,
Versailles

Jewel Cabinet by J-F Schwerdfeger, *p44*:
Château de Versailles,
Versailles

Empress Josephine's Bed, *p68*:
Musée National de
Malmaison,
Rueil-Malmaison

Mechanical Desk by Giovanni Socci, *p132*:
Musée National du Château
de Fontainebleau,
Fontainebleau

GERMANY

Bureau Cabinet by David Roentgen, *p40*:
Schloss Köpenick, Berlin

ITALY

Bureau Cabinet, *p18*:
Palazzo Quirinale, Rome

Italian Throne Seat by Antonio Corradini, *p30*:
Palazzo Ca Rezzonico, Venice

SPAIN

Dressing Table and Chairs by Antoni Gaudí, *p172*:
Museo Gaudí, Parc Güell,
Barcelona

SWEDEN

Commode Bed by Georg Haupt, *p124*:
Royal Castle, Stockholm

UNITED KINGDOM

The Sea Dog Table, *p20*:
Hardwick Hall, Doe Lea,
Nr Chesterfield, Derbyshire

The Knole Silver Suite, *p26*:
Knole, Sevenoaks, Kent

Casket on Stand by Pietro Piffetti, *p28*:
Victoria & Albert Museum,
Cromwell Road,
London

The Murray Cabinet by John Channon, *p36*:
Temple Newsam House,
Leeds, West Yorkshire

The Dolphin Suite, *p46*:
The Royal Pavilion, Brighton,
East Sussex

Chinoiserie Bed by William and John Linnell, *p56*:
Victoria & Albert Museum,
Cromwell Road,
London

Giltwood Sofas by William and John Linnell, *p58*:
Kedleston Hall, Derbyshire

The Duke of Atholl's Medal Cabinet, *p62*:
Blair Castle, Blair Atholl,
Pitlochry, Tayside, Scotland

Indo-Portugese Table, *p80*:
Victoria & Albert Museum,
Cromwell Road,
London

The Coronation Chair, *p82*:
Westminster Abbey,
London

Nerli-Morelli Cassoni, *p84*:
Courtauld Institute,
Somerset House, Strand,
London

French Ebony Cabinet, *p90*:
The Royal Collection,
Windsor Castle, Windsor,
Berkshire

Lignum Vitae Cabinets, *p92*:
The Royal Collection,
Windsor Castle, Windsor,
Berkshire

Boulle Marquetry Cabinet on Stand, *p94*:
Wallace Collection,
Manchester Square,
London

The Venus and Diana Commodes, *p100*:
Osterley Park, Isleworth,
Middlesex

Pietre Dure Commode by Martin Carlin, *p104*:
The Royal Collection,
Buckingham Palace, London

Sofa by John Henry Belter, *p108*:
Victoria & Albert Museum,
Cromwell Road, London

Mechanical Desk, *p114*:
Waddesdon Manor,
Nr Aylesbury,
Buckinghamshire

Sleeping Chair, *p116*:
Ham House, Ham, Surrey

Table à la Bourgogne by J-F Oeben, *p118*:
Luton Hoo, Luton,
Bedfordshire

Metamorphic Library Steps, *p120*:
Harewood House,
Harewood, Leeds;
Temple Newsam House,
Leeds, West Yorkshire;
Christ Church College,
Oxford

French Cylinder-top Desk, *p126*:
Waddesdon Manor,
Nr Aylesbury,
Buckinghamshire

Savonnerie Screen, *p146*:
Waddesdon Manor
Nr Aylesbury,
Buckinghamshire

Paper Filigree Cabinet, *p150*:
Lady Lever Art Gallery,
Port Sunlight Village,
Wirral, Merseyside

Faux Bamboo Furniture, *p152*:
The Royal Pavilion,
Brighton, Sussex

The Table of the Grand Commanders, *p154*:
The Royal Collection,
Buckingham Palace, London

Papier Mâché Bedroom Suite, *p160*:
Lotherton Hall, Aberfold,
Leeds, West Yorkshire

Antler Furniture, *p162*:
Osborne House,
East Cowes, Isle of Wight

UNITED STATES

Japanned Boston Highboy, *p54*:
Bayou Bend, 1 Westcott
Street, Houston, Texas

Block-fronted Desk Bookcase, *p64*:
Bayou Bend, 1 Westcott
Street, Houston, Texas

Baltimore Lady's Desk, *p66*:
Winterthur Museum,
Winterthur, Delaware

Shaker Built-in Storage, *p72*:
Church Dwelling House,
Canterbury Shaker Village,
Canterbury,
New Hampshire

Frank Lloyd Wright Chairs, *p76*:
Darwin D Martin House,
Buffalo, New York

Chest-on-chest by Lemon and McIntire, *p98*:
Museum of Fine Arts
Boston, 465 Huntington Av,
Boston, Massachusetts

Commode by John and Thomas Seymour, *p102*:
Museum of Fine Arts
Boston, 465 Huntington Av,
Boston, Massachusetts

Mechanical Table by Martin Carlin, *p130*:
Frick Museum, New York

Trompe l'oeil Furniture by Wendell Castle, *p178*:
Houston Museum of Fine
Art, Houston, Texas

Bibliography

Alcouffe, D, *Mobilier du Musée du Louvre* (2 vols)

Beard, G and Goodison, J, *English Furniture*, 1962

Bellaigue, Geoffrey de, *The James A de Rothschild Collection at Waddesdon Manor*, 1974; *Carlton House: The Past Glories of George IV's Palace*, 1991

Bjerkoe, Ethel Hall, *The Cabinet Makers of America*, 1957

Chevallier, Bernard, *Malmaison Château et Domaine des Origines à 1904*, 1989

Coleridge, Anthony, *Chippendale Furniture*, 1968

Collard, Frances, *Regency Furniture*, 1985

Comstock, H, *American Furniture, Seventeenth, Eighteenth and Nineteenth Century Styles*, 1962

Dejean, Philippe, *Bugatti: Carlo, Rembrandt, Ettore, Jean*, 1982

Deschamps, Madeleine, *Empire*, 1994

Downs, J, *American Furniture in Winterthur*, 1952

Fastnedge, R, *Sheraton Furniture*, 1962

Brière, G, *Furniture of the 18th Century (Frick Collection)*, 1955

Gilbert, Christopher, *Furniture at Temple Newsam House and Lotherton Hall*, 1978; *The Life and Work of Thomas Chippendale*, 1978

Gilbert, Christopher and Murdoch, Tessa, *John Channon and Brass-inlaid Furniture*, 1993

Girouard, Mark, *Hardwick Hall, Derbyshire*, 1976

Gonzalez-Palacios, A, *The Art of Mosaics, A Selection from the Gilbert Collection (Los Angeles County Museum)*, 1982

Grandjean, Serge, *Empire Furniture*, 1966

Groer, Leon de, *Decorative Arts in Europe 1790–1850*, 1986

Guisti, Anna Maria, *Pietre Dure: Hardstone in Furniture and Decorations*, 1992

Hanks, DA, *Frank Lloyd Wright, Preserving an Architectural Heritage*, 1989

Hardy, J and Tomlin, M, *Osterley Park House*, 1985

Haslam, Malcolm, *The Amazing Bugattis*, 1979

Hayward, Helena, ed, *World Furniture*, 1969; *William and John Linnell*, 1980

Heinz, TA, *Frank Lloyd Wright, Interiors and Furniture*, 1994

Himmelheber, Georg, *Biedermeier Furniture*, 1974

Hipkiss, Edwin J, *The M & M Karolik Collection in the Museum of Fine Art Boston*, 1941

Huth, Hans, *Roentgen Furniture*, 1974

Jackson Stops, Gervase, *The Treasure Houses of Britain, Five Hundred Years of Private Patronage and Art Collecting*, 1985; *The English Country House: A Grand Tour*, 1985

Jervis, Simon, *Printed Furniture Designs before 1650*, 1974

Ledoux, Lebard D, *Le Mobilier Français du XIX Siècle; Dictionnaire des Ebénistes et Menuisiers*, 1984

Lunsingh Scheurleer, TH, "Novels in Ebony" in *Journal of the Warburg and Courtauld Institute*, 1956

Macquoid, Percy and Edwards, Ralph, *The Dictionary of English Furniture* (3 vols), 1954

Miller, N, *Heavenly Caves, Reflections on Garden Grottos*, 1982

Molesworth, HD, *Three Centuries of Furniture*, 1969

Montgomery, CG, *American Furniture of the Federal Period*, 1967

Musgrave, C, *Adam, Hepplewhite and other Neoclassical Furniture*, 1966; *Regency Furniture*, 1961

Myerson, Jeremy, *Makepeace – A spirit of Adventure in Craft and Design*, 1995

National Trust, *Ham House*, 1995

Ostergard, DE, ed, *Bentwood and Metal Furniture 1850–1946*, 1987

Payne, Christopher, *Nineteenth Century European Furniture*, 1984; *Sotheby's Concise Encyclopedia of Furniture*, ed, 1989

Pradère, A, *French Furniture Makers from Louis XIV to the Revolution*, 1990

Percier, Charles and Fontaine, Pierre-François Léonard, *Recueil de Décorations Intérieures...*, 1812

Reynies, N, *Le Mobilier Domestique* (2 vols), 1987

Riccardi-Cubitt, Monique, *The Art of the Cabinet*, 1992

Rieman, TD and Burks, JM, *The Complete Book of Shaker Furniture*, 1993

Sheraton, Thomas, *The Cabinet-Maker and Upholsterer's Drawing-Book*, 1794

Taragin, DS, *Furniture by Wendell Castle*, 1989

Thornton, P and Tomalin, M, *The Furnishing and Decoration of Ham House*, 1980

Verlet, P, *French Royal Furniture*, 1963

Warren, D, *American Furniture at Bayou Bend*, 1975

Watson, FJB, *Furniture,* Wallace Collection Catalogue, 1956

Zerbst, Rainer, *Antoni Gaudí*, 1993

Index

Index

Acknowledgements

The author would particularly like to thank:

Ruth Kennedy, for without her this book would not have been written, Tim Gosling, for giving continual inspiration, and everyone at David Linley Furniture for advice, encouragement, enthusiasm and endless cups of delicious coffee. To Janet Gleeson, who has been such an excellent catalyst to this book, a pleasure to work with for her tireless research and hard work, and from whom an enormous amount has been learnt – thank you.

The author and publisher would like to thank the following individuals and institutions for their generous help:

Mrs E Adamthwaite and the Trustees of Greenwich Hospital; Jane Anderson, Blair Castle; Heather Libson, Arenski; Stella Beddoe, Royal Pavilion, Brighton; Sir Geoffrey de Bellaigue, Director of the Royal Collection; Dr R Bauer and Dr M Leithe-Jasper, Kunsthistorisches Museum, Vienna; Helen Braham, Courtauld Institute; Michael K Brown, Bayou Bend; Yves Carlier, Musée National du Château de Fontainebleau, Wendell Castle; Shane Gleeson; Carlton Hobbs and Edward Bridges; John Hobbs; Viscount Folkestone; Peter Hughes, Wallace Collection; Brock Jobe, Winterthur Museum; John Makepeace; Bryan Milton, Custodian of the Wernher collection, Luton Hoo; Tessa Murdoch and James Yorke, Victoria & Albert Museum; Christopher Payne; Peter Petrou and Janine Haberman; Brigadier Pownall; Orlando Rock; Christie's; Bernard Rondot, Ministère de la Culture Malmaison; John Smith, Mallett; Gerald WR Ward, Museum of Fine Arts, Boston; Charles Wheeler-Carmichael; Dr Christian Witt-Dorring, MAK Museum, Vienna; Lucy Wood, Lady Lever Art Gallery.

Picture acknowledgements: 2 Bridgeman Art Library (Index, Museo Gaudí, Barcelona); 5 Waddesdon Manor, The National Trust (Hugo Maertens); 6 *bottom* Courtesy of the Ca' Rezzonico (Angelo Hornak), *top* The Museum of Fine Arts, Houston; The Bayou Bend Collection, gift of Miss Ima Hogg; 7 *top* Courtesy of Carlton Hobbs (John Hammond), *right* The Museum of Fine Arts, Houston; Museum purchase with funds provided by Roy M. Huffington, Inc., *bottom* Private collection,England; 8 Scala; 9 David Linley Furniture Limited (Patrick Steel); 10 David Linley Furniture Limited (John Hammond); 11 Greenwich Hospital; 12 The Royal Collection Copyright 1996 Her Majesty Queen Elizabeth II; 13 *The Cabinet-Maker and Upholsterer's Drawing-Book* by Thomas Sheraton; 14 Leeds Museums and Galleries (Temple Newsam House); 15 Bridgeman Art Library, by courtesy of Trustees of the Victoria & Albert Museum; 16 Réunion des Musées Nationaux (M Coppola); 17 David Linley Furniture Limited; 18 Scala; 20 *top* National Trust Photographic Library, *centre* Robert Harding Picture Library (Adam Woolfitt), *bottom* National Trust Photographic Library (John Bethell); 21 The Interior Archive (C Simon Sykes); 22 *top* AKG London (Erich Lessing), *bottom* Copyright Reed International Books Ltd, courtesy of John Hobbs (John Hammond); 23, 24/25 Copyright Reed International Books Ltd, courtesy of John Hobbs (John Hammond); 26 *top* The Interior Archive (C Simon Sykes), *bottom* National Trust Photographic Library (John Hammond); 27 *bottom* The Interior Archive (C Simon Sykes), *top* National Trust Photographic Library (Andreas von Einsiedel); 28 *top* Palazzo Quirinale, *bottom* By courtesy of the Board of Trustees of the Victoria & Albert Museum; 29 By courtesy of the Board of Trustees of the Victoria & Albert Museum; 30 Bridgeman Art Library (Ca' Rezzonico, Venice), *bottom* Angelo Hornak; 31 Angelo Hornak; 32 *top* Bridgeman Art Library (private collection), *bottom* Christie's Images; 33, 34 Christie's Images; 35 Country Life Picture Library; 36/37 Leeds Museums and Galleries (Temple Newsam House); 38 *top* Bridgeman Art Library (Giraudon), *centre and bottom* Réunion des Musées Nationaux; 39 Réunion des Musées Nationaux; 40/41 Staatliche Museen zu Berlin – Preussischer Kulturbesitz, Kunstgewerbemuseum (Pierre Abboud); 42 *top* Réunion des Musées Nationaux, *bottom* The Royal Collection Copyright 1996 Her Majesty Queen Elizabeth II; 43 The Royal Collection Copyright 1996 Her Majesty Queen Elizabeth II; 44 *top* Bridgeman Art Library (Giraudon), *bottom* Réunion des Musées Nationaux; 45 *bottom* Bibliothèque Nationale,

top Réunion des Musées Nationaux; 46 *top* Copyright Reed International Books Ltd (Tim Ridley), *bottom* Courtesy of Brigadier John Pownall; 47, 48/49 Copyright Reed International Books Ltd (Tim Ridley); 50 *top* David Linley Furniture Limited, *bottom Dictionary of English Furniture, Volume One* by Ralph Edwards; 51 David Linley Furniture Limited (Patrick Steel); 52 Osterreichisches Museum fur Angewandte Kunst; 54/55 The Museum of Fine Arts, Houston; The Bayou Bend Collection, gift of Miss Ima Hogg; 56 *bottom English Furniture Woodwork Decoration etc, during the 18th Century* by TA Strange, *top* By courtesy of the Trustees of the Victoria & Albert Museum; 57 Bridgeman Art Library, by courtesy of the Board of Trustees of the Victoria & Albert Museum; 58 *top* By courtesy of the Trustees of the Victoria & Albert Museum, *bottom* National Trust Photographic Library (Andrew Haslam); 59 National Trust Photographic Library (Andrew Haslam); 60 *top* Country Life Picture Library, *bottom* Gerstenfeld Collection; 61 Christie's Images; 62 *top* Robert Harding Picture Library (Simon Harris), *bottom* Copyright Reed International Books Ltd (Ronald Weir); 63 *top* Fratelli Alinari, *bottom* Copyright Reed International Books Ltd (Ronald Weir); 64/65 The Museum of Fine Arts, Houston; The Bayou Bend Collection, gift of Miss Ima Hogg; 66 Courtesy, Winterthur Museum; 67 *top* Bridgeman Art Library (Courtesy, Winterthur Museum), *bottom The Cabinet-Maker and Upholsterer's Drawing-Book* by Thomas Sheraton; 68 *top* Joe Cornish, *bottom* Réunion des Musées Nationaux; 69 Fritz von der Schulenberg/The Interior Archive; 70 Réunion des Musées Nationaux; 71 *bottom* Bridgeman Art Library (Giraudon/Château de Versailles), *right* Royal Institute of British Architects; 72 *top* Bridgeman Art Library (private collection), *bottom* Fritz von der Schulenburg/The Interior Archive; 73 Fritz von der Schulenburg/The Interior Archive; 74/75 Tim Rieman; 76 *top* Photograph by Thomas A Heinz (1994 copyright Thomas A Heinz), *bottom* Corbis/Bettmann (UPI); 77 Photograph by Thomas A Heinz (1994 Copyright Thomas A Heinz); 78 *left* David Linley Furniture Limited, *centre* Robert Harding Picture Library, *right* Tony Stone Images (Fred George); 79 David Linley Furniture Limited (John Hammond); 80/81 By courtesy of the Board of Trustees of the Victoria & Albert Museum; 82 Bridgeman Art Library (Bradford Art Galleries and Museums), *bottom* By courtesy of The Master and Fellows of Corpus Christi College, Cambridge (The Parker Library); 83 Courtesy of Dean and Chapter of Westminster (Angelo Hornak); 84/85, 86/87 Courtauld Institute Galleries, London (AC Cooper Ltd); 88 *top* Copyright Reed International Books Ltd (Robin Saker), *bottom* Bridgeman Art Library (Kunsthistorisches Musuem, Vienna); 89 Copyright Reed International Books Ltd (Robin Saker); 90/91 The Royal Collection Copyright 1996 Her Majesty Queen Elizabeth II; 92 *top* Hulton Deutsch Collection, *bottom* The Royal Collection Copyright 1996 Her Majesty Queen Elizabeth II; 93 The Royal Collection Copyright 1996 Her Majesty Queen Elizabeth II; 94/95 Reproduced by the kind permission of the Trustees of the Wallace Collection (John Hammond); 96 *left* Reproduced by the kind permission of the Trustees of the Wallace Collection (John Hammond), *right* Buccleuch Recreational Enterprises Ltd, (by permission of the Duke of Buccleuch and Queensberry KT); 97 Reproduced by the kind permission of the Trustees of the Wallace Collection (John Hammond); 98 *top* M & M Karolik Collection of Eighteenth Century American Arts courtesy Museum of Fine Arts, Boston, *bottom The Gentleman and Cabinet-Maker's Director* by Thomas Chippendale; 99 M & M Karolik Collection of Eighteenth Century American Arts courtesy Museum of Fine Arts, Boston; 100/101 Courtesy of the Trustees of the Victoria & Albert Museum; 102 *top* Mary Evans Picture Library, *bottom* M & M Karolik Collection of Eighteenth Century American Arts courtesy Museum of Fine Arts, Boston; 103 M & M Karolik Collection of Eighteenth Century American Arts courtesy Museum of Fine Arts, Boston; 104 *top* The Royal Collection Copyright 1996 Her Majesty Queen Elizabeth II, *bottom* Bibliothèque Nationale de France; 105 The Royal Collection Copyright 1996 Her Majesty Queen Elizabeth II; 106 *top* Copyright Reed International Books Ltd, courtesy of Carlton Hobbs (John Hammond), *bottom* Courtesy of Carlton Hobbs (John Hammond); 107 Courtesy of Carlton Hobbs (John Hammond); 108 *top* The Museum of Fine Arts,

Houston (Bayou Bend Collection), *bottom* US Dept of Commerce; 109 By courtesy of the Trustees of the Victoria & Albert Museum; 110 John Makepeace Furniture Studio (Mike Murless/Farquharson Murless); 111 *top* John Makepeace Furniture Studio (Jonathan Lovekin), *bottom* John Makepeace Furniture Studio; 112 David Linley Furniture Limited (Patrick Steel); 113 David Linley Furniture Limited (Patrick Steel); 114 Waddesdon Manor, The National Trust (Hugo Maertens); 116 *top* By courtesy of the Trustees of the Victoria & Albert Museum, *bottom* By courtesy of the Trustees of the Victoria & Albert Museum (Ken Jackson); 117 By courtesy of the Trustees of the Victoria & Albert Museum; 118 *top* Wernher Collection/Luton Hoo Foundation (Shelagh Collingwood), *bottom* Bibliothèque Nationale de France; 119 Wernher Collection/Luton Hoo Foundation (Shelagh Collingwood); 120 Stahovska Knihovna, Klaster premonstratu na Strahove (Jan Parez); 121 *left* By courtesy of the Trustees of the Victoria & Albert Museum, *right* Leeds Museums and Galleries (Temple Newsam House); 122 Trinity College, Oxford (Woolwich Building Society); 123 Harewood House Trust Ltd; 124 Fritz von der Schulenburg/The Interior Archive; 125 Kungl Husgeradskammaren, Drottningholm Palace, The Royal Collections (Hakan Lind); 126 Waddesdon Manor, The National Trust (AC Cooper); 127 Waddesdon Manor, The National Trust (Eost & MacDonald); 128 Waddesdon Manor, The National Trust (John Freeman); 129 Waddesdon Manor, The National Trust (AC Cooper); 130/131 Copyright The Frick Collection, New York; 132/133 Réunion des Musées Nationaux; 134 *top* By courtesy of the Trustees of the Victoria & Albert Museum, *bottom* Robert Harding Picture Library; 135 Private collection, England; 136/137 Copyright Reed International Books Ltd, courtesy of Mr Wu (Tim Ridley); 138 *top* Phillips Auctioneers, *bottom* British Library; 139 Phillips Auctioneers; 140/141 WG Bosshard; 142 *top* Devonshire Collection, reproduced by kind permission of the Chatsworth Settlement Trustees, *bottom* David Linley Furniture Limited /by kind permission of Alfred Dunhill (Steve Wakeham at Sutton Cooper); 143 David Linley Furniture Limited/by kind permission of Alfred Dunhill (Steve Wakeham at Sutton Cooper); 144 *left* David Linley Furniture Limited/by kind permission of Alfred Dunhill (Steve Wakeham at Sutton Cooper), *right* David Linley Furniture Limited; 145 *left* David Linley Furniture Limited, *right* David Linley Furniture Limited/by kind permission of Alfred Dunhill (Steve Wakeham at Sutton Cooper); 146 Waddesdon Manor, The National Trust (Roberton); 148/149 Angelo Hornak; 150/151 National Museums & Galleries on Merseyside (Lady Lever Art Gallery); 152 *left* Royal Pavilion Art Galleries and Museums, Brighton, *right* The Royal Collection Copyright 1996 Her Majesty Queen Elizabeth II (Tim Ridley); 153 The Royal Collection Copyright 1996 Her Majesty Queen Elizabeth II (Tim Ridley); 154/155 The Royal Collection Copyright 1996 Her Majesty Queen Elizabeth II; 156 *top* Bridgeman Art Library (Giraudon, Château de Versailles, France), *bottom* Hulton Deutsch Collection; 157 Kunsthistorisches Museum; 158 *top* Hulton Deutsch Collection, *bottom* The Royal Collection Copyright 1996 Her Majesty Queen Elizabeth II; 159 The Royal Collection Copyright 1996 Her Majesty Queen Elizabeth II; 160/161 Leeds Museums and Galleries (Lotherton Hall); 162 English Heritage; 163 The Royal Collection Copyright 1996 Her Majesty Queen Elizabeth II; 164 *top* Mallett & Son (Antiques) Ltd, *bottom* Mallett & Son (Antiques) Ltd (The Birmingham Museums and Art Gallery); 165 Mallett & Son (Antiques) Ltd; 166 *top* By kind permission of the Marquess of Tavistock and the Trustees of the Bedford Estate, *centre and bottom* Copyright Reed International Books Ltd, courtesy of Peter Petrou (Tim Imrie); 167, 168/169, 170 Copyright Reed International Books Ltd, courtesy of Peter Petrou (Tim Imrie); 171 *top* Arenski (Tim Imrie), *bottom* Carlton Hobbs (Tim Imrie); 172 Bridgeman Art Library (Index/Palacio Güell, Barcelona); 173 Bridgeman Art Library (Index/Museo Gaudí, Barcelona); 174 Bridgeman Art Library (Index/Güell Family Collection, Spain); 175 Bridgeman Art Library (Index/Palacio Güell, Barcelona); 176 *top* Philippe Garner, *bottom* Sotheby's (London); 177 Sotheby's (London); 178 *top* Wendell Castle, Inc, *bottom* The Museum of Fine Arts, Houston; Museum purchase with funds provided by Roy M. Huffington, Inc.; 179 Wendell Castle, Inc; 180/181, 182/183 David Linley Furniture Limited (Patrick Steel).